NEVER STAY SILENT

Silence Is Crippling

KAELEE I. MILLER

Never Stay Silent
Silence Is Crippling
by Kaelee I. Miller

Printed in the United States of America.

ISBN 9781498465021

www.xulonpress.com

Table of Contents

Dedication

I dedicate this book to the women who has shown me that Life has no limits…. Just because life goes wrong at times doesn't mean life is over, it just means you have to push harder. Thank you Jean Smith for allowing me to express myself. Thank you for reaching out to me and holding my hand thru some very dark times. I also say thank you for being there when I was very successful. Even though you cannot see me you had a special way to connecting with me. Thru your disability you have shown me that my dreams can actually be a reality. Thank You

Chapter 1

"Do you trust me?" Manny asked as he sat me on the couch.

"Yeah," I said.

"Are you sure?" he asked.

"Yeah," I said.

"Okay, we're going to do these classes a little different, and it's a secret."

I knew what those words meant, and I knew what was coming. I had just finished going to court for being molested by my mother's boyfriend. But there was nothing I could do. I was alone in the house with him and he was bigger than me.

He started to unbutton my blouse.

"No!" I pushed him away. But he pushed me down on the couch and pulled the rest of my clothes off. I was naked and exposed to him. He stopped and looked at me with a smile and then started to kiss me all over my body. He ate me out.

"You taste like fruit. Did you eat anything fruity today because you taste like you did."

"I had a banana," I quietly responded. I don't even think he heard me. He forced his fingers inside me, two and then three, back and forth, harder and harder. Then he forced himself onto me and stuck his penis inside of me.

It wasn't the first time a man had touched me inappropriately, my mother had dated several men who had fondled my breasts or fingered me. But I had never had sex before. I lost my virginity that day. And I stayed silent because I didn't believe anyone could or would do anything for me.

As Manny spread himself on top of me, finishing his business, it suddenly all became clear to me. I understood why he wanted me, a sixth grade girl, to teach him English. Why my mother was so insistent that I go to his house alone for the lessons. Why he was willing to pay so much for them. He rolled off of me and pulled up his pants. Then he grabbed a baby wipe and gently wiped all the semen off my stomach, in an almost loving gesture. He had to make sure I was all cleaned up. All I could do was lay there and wonder how my mother could do this to me. Why? Was money really that important to her?

"Get up, put your clothes on," Manny said. He knew English, he didn't need lessons. "The lesson for today is done. You are a good teacher. Don't tell anyone about what happens here during our lessons, okay?"

I nodded as I put on my navy blue school pants, my training bra and my white button up shirt, my black patent leather shoes. It didn't even last long enough to mess up my hair.

"I want you to come back for another lesson tomorrow, understand?"

I understood. I understood more now than I did before. This was what my life was to be now. Daily English lessons with Manny.

I went back across the street to my house to do my homework. Manny followed me, into my house and into my room. He picked me up and put me on his lap, monitoring me to make sure I never told anyone. I didn't tell anyone for a long time. I stayed silent.

I have learned over the years that staying silent is the worst thing you can do. It will slowly kill you from the inside out. Learning to never stay silent has been the hardest lesson of all for me, but it has saved my life. I want to share this with the world in the hopes that it will encourage others to speak up, to tell their story. To never stay silent.

My twin brother Jeffrey and I were born on July 25, 1986 at Lawrence General Hospital in Lawrence, Ma. We were full term babies which doesn't happen much with twins. Our sister Jessica, who shared our mother but not our father, was four years old. Our father was an immigrant from the Dominican Republic. He also had a child from a previous relationship, our brother William Jr. who was nine months older than we were.

My father and mother met through my mother's cousin at a night club. They were only together for four to five months before my mother got pregnant. She did not know she was carrying twins until she was six months along. I was the surprise twin! Their relationship ended as soon as it started. My father had many relationships and did not want to commit to one person. He wanted to play the field and not deal with what he got himself into.

Our father and mother argued a lot about money. For a long time my father would give my mother money to take care of us, and my mother would take the money and spend it on other things such as her boyfriends. My father soon caught on to her games and stopped giving my mother money. Instead, he would bring her whatever she asked for. He would buy us clothes, medicine, milk, or whatever else we needed, and brought it that to her instead of giving her money. My mother obviously did not like that, and began to play games with my father. She would tell him that we were not his children, so my father began to doubt if we were his or not.

My father played games as well. He would pick us up and bring us to all of his girlfriend's houses. I usd to get so angry because he would do so much more for his girlfriend's children than us. I felt robbed of my father's love and attention.

Our older brother William Jr. lived with our father. I was so jealous. My father's main girlfriend Ramona, who is now his wife, took care of him. I felt like he had everything. He had love. He was raised with our culture and learned a second language. He experienced normal childhood things such as Little League. He was able to travel to the Dominican Republic and got to know our family.

Jeffery and I did not have that opportunity. Our mother took it from us. We never were involved in extra-curricular activities like William was. If it cost money we did not get to experience it. There were some activities I was able to experience like playing volleyball at the YWCA. I got to be involved in that because it didn't cost anything. I also played basketball and got to be a cheerleader at one point. I shined, and won awards for being the most spirited. I remember my mother sitting there saying "that's my girl" as if she had anything to do with it. I was happy at the moment but inside I knew my mother was just playing the game.

My mother always showed up for things. She gloated about anything that would give her some kind of attention. It didn't have to be about her but she always made sure her presence was well known. She worked hard to appear to be a good mom to outsiders while also diverting all the positive attention to herself.

The abuse started early. As a young child I learned that I had to walk on eggshells around my mother. She was and still is a bomb ready to explode. My siblings and I knew by the sound of her voice or the way she walked through the door if we were going to get it or not. I knew that whatever I did was not going to be good enough so I always prepared myself for a smack or a beating.

I remember waking one afternoon from a nap when I was about six or seven years old. I was hungry so I decided to make a peanut butter and jelly sandwich. My mother had just finished mopping the kitchen floor and I was walking on it, not knowing any better. She heard me and came into the kitchen.

"What the fuck are you doing? I just mopped the kitchen! Can't you see I mopped the kitchen floor?" Before I knew it, she had jumped on me and was hitting me. She grabbed me by my pony tail and threw me around the kitchen. I was so upset and scared, I ended up wetting myself. This enraged her even more.

"Take off your clothes! Get out! Leave my house! Only pigs pee outside! Only pigs pee on themselves!"

She opened the door and pushed me into the hallway. I sat there naked, crunched up into a ball, crying. The kids from downstairs came up and wanted me to come with them. I was so afraid I didn't dare to move. She then whipped open the door and made me come inside as the kids ran downstairs.

"Wipe up your pee you pig!" I went back to bed hungry. I never got to have that peanut butter and jelly sandwich.

There were good times too. My twin and I shared a bed room. We lived in an apartment on Butler St. in Lawrence, on the second floor. We had a play room outside the apartment in a storage room where we played for hours. I had all of my dolls and Barbie's and he had his match box cars and race tracks. Downstairs from us there was a family of four, two girls and two boys. One of the boys O-jay was about the same age as Jeffery and I. He became my childhood sweet heart. We would go to play outside in our back yard which was an empty lot filled with high grass. We would play hide and seek. We would run as if we were in the country running around in big fields with not a care in the world. We would climb trees, sheds, anything that we were not afraid of. We had no fear when we were outside. Sometimes we would bumper ski, where we jumped on the bumper of a car and hold on to the back while it drove down the street on back of the ice cream trucks. The ice cream man would open the back and throw ice cold water on us for us to let go. Now as an adult I realize how foolish we were. We were so lucky that we didn't get hurt or worse killed.

Then came the day we moved to Berkeley Street. My mother took us to the new apartment and we got to pick out our own rooms. We were so excited. We had our own back yard. We were going to be able to ride our bikes. Everything was great. Maybe now things were going to be different. And they were, at first. It was wonderful. And then reality started sinking in and I realized we were wrong. Berkeley Street was hell.

Jeffrey and I celebrated our last birthday together in that house when we turned nine. Every year after that I would be at camp, or we were apart for some other reason. I will never forget that day. Jeffrey got dressed before I did, because I didn't get in the shower fast enough, so I got a beating. My mother always viewed him as the better twin, even though I stayed out of trouble more and did well in school. Despite my beating, I had so much fun. I had on a white princess dress that my Dad bought me. There were so many people there.

My mother would do anything for money. Even if it meant putting her children in danger she did it. We soon had a growing family, mostly men who were gang members who and pimps. She allowed them to use our house as their stomping grounds.

They would bring their prostitutes in and out of our home. My mother eventually put my brother and me in one room in order for the pimps to use a room for their business. As long as she was making some kind of profit she did it. She never cared of for the danger that we were in. My twin and I would find used needles in the back yard all the time. These pimps that were our "brothers" would always have people over which meant that there was always alcohol and drugs. My mother didn't see any harm in allowing this. These "brothers" of ours never hurt any of us but they were dangerous. They were known by the police. I remember one of them being shot in his leg. My mother knew this but for some reason she rationalized it to be okay.

The beatings began to increase on Berkeley Street. My siblings and I knew when it was coming just by the sound of our mother's voice or appearance. She usually began by yelling. If she was sitting she would throw anything that was within reach. If she decided to get up from where she was sitting we knew we were in for it and we would run or try to get away. She would hit us with belts, and punch us on our backs or stomachs as if we were grown men. She had no problems slapping us in the face, throwing us against walls, or breaking brooms and mops over our backs. She would grab anything she could and she became like an animal. At some point she started to choke us. She did this to my twin more often than me. He would be turning blue and she would not let go. Someone would have to physically pull her off of him.

I remember one time we had a grease fire and being so young we did not know what to do. Jessica was cooking dinner and Jeffrey turned the stove on. We did not know that there was grease in the stove and it caught on fire. We threw water on it, trying to put it out, but it only got worse. My mother ran into the kitchen and put the fire out, but by then the fire department had been alerted. They came and made sure that everything was okay. After they left, the kitchen table was flipped over and Jessica and I got beat. Our mother punched us. She hit us with the broom and some pots and pans until she felt like she was done. Even though Jeffery was the one who turned the oven on, he didn't get in trouble.

My mother favored boys. My twin was her only son. Jeffrey still got beat, but not as much and he always had more privileges. My sister and I were the scum of the earth and she made sure that we knew it. She would swear at us and call us bitches, or tell us that we were nobodies. She would say things like she never wanted us especially to me. She wished me dead more times than I can count. At eleven years old I would cry out to God on my knees," God if you love me please take me home with you." I would be so angry and confused when I would see my friend's moms treat them with such love. They really cared about them. I didn't understand why and I thought that I was the one who was wrong. That there was something about me that made my mother so angry.

She would always brag about me in front of other people. She used to tell people that I was her smart one. That she didn't have to stay on top of me. How proud of me she was. But at home it was a different story. I was the one she never wanted, I was the bad one for being born. I was different and she knew it. She knew that I was going to be someone great. That I was the one who was going to better than she ever was and she couldn't deal with it. She worked really hard for me to think or believe that I was going to be a nobody.

Chapter 2

The innocence of Little Girls

Little girls are so beautiful. They love to play and copy their environment around them. They love to dress up, and put on make-up, cook in the kitchen and make with tons of food. They like to play mother, teacher, baby, so on and so forth. The one thing that little girls want to do is to please the people around them. It does not matter if it's their parents, family, friends, siblings, or teachers... So when your mother one day suggest for you to go help a "family friend" learn English, and she tells you that you will get paid money for the lessons. As her daughter, you say ok (even if you are flunking English in school)...You do it because you want to please her. You think that it would help her love you more so you do it. ...Why? Why would your own mother send you out to lose your innocence for money and then call you a liar!! Why could you not join after school programs because you had a duty to fulfill that duty you were no good!!" You are a bitch, cunt; I hate you; you are no good, you selfish." Why was the innocence of this little girl taken away by her own mother?

Exposed

My soul is exposed open to slander, malice, love, joy, and confusion

Where to go with it all; I don't know

Wait GOD?

How can I, I'm so unworthy

I'm totally exposed to the things around me and it's hurting me

Forcing myself to be around the one who hurts me

15

If she only knew the pain she causes

It hurts me to know that she thinks that all of it is so funny

She laughs all the time and makes jokes

I'm so glad she thinks selling her daughter to a man who took her innocence away is funny

Or how it's funny how she used to hit or I mean beat me

Watching my brother turn blue so many times does not give me good family memories

Or how about I love you, go next door if not you're selfish or you a bitch

I'm hurting and exposed to the elements around me

I'm so scared

Where to turn, who to call, what to do

I'm crying inside and inside are lies of my desire to be set free

Today I'm sad tomorrow a new day for right now a prayer to get through…

*M*y grandmother on my mother's side passed away on January 3, 2007. She and I were very close. I missed her passing by ten minutes. During the last five years of her life, I would visit and paint her nails while she told me stories of all the things she had gone through in her life. Those secrets aren't mine to share, but she understood me in ways she didn't even realize. My grandmother was a very strong woman, and she did what she had to do in order to survive. She was a very influential figure in my life and I will always love the memory of the conversations we shared.

One of the most important things my grandmother shared with me was the story of her salvation. My grandmother was a Christian and she gave me a piece of her God. I remember praying with her each time I visited.

There were a lot of good things that happened during my childhood as well, things that gave me hope for a better life. One of those things was going camping at my Uncle Henry's house in the White Mountains. It was a four hour drive from our house and we would go for two weeks at a time. It was magical to go to Uncle Henry and Aunty Elma's house. The beatings didn't stop, but they had to be planned more because my mother did not want my uncle Henry to know. This alone made the time more enjoyable.

My mother had a fire engine red minivan that fit seven people. We would stuff as much stuff into and on top of the van as possible. As we arrived at Uncle Henry's we broke free from the van like wild animals. Shrieks of excitement filled the air! Aunty and Uncle gave us lots of hugs and kisses.

It was so much fun when we were kids. Uncle Henry created a pond in the back yard and named it Henry's pond. It was filled with fish. He had his own row boat that we played with. He also had a huge lawn. He would take his lawn mower and hook up a topless trailer to the back of it. He would put hay in it and take us on hay rides. As we got older we got to drive the mower ourselves. He had his own chicken and turkey coop in the yard. As children it never occurred to us where dinner came from, but I do remember that they always made amazing chicken and turkey soup! There was a small marsh on the backside of his land which led over into the camping grounds and there was a wooden plank that we crossed over. It was paradise. There were campers to sleep in and sometimes we put up tents. There was a fire pit that we cooked on and roasted marshmallows or used to stay warm on those cold summer nights.

We always got busy right away. My twin and I would run through the woods to get fire wood, not going too far for fear of wild animals. The older adults would put ropes and tarps up to create a shower. The van got unloaded faster than it was packed. Everything had its place. The coolers went by the fire pit. Suitcases went into campers. The best thing about camping was the magic tire swing uncle Henry hung up for us. As soon as our chores were done we went for the swing! As dinner approached on our first night we crossed back over the marsh to aunty and uncle's house for dinner. Into the house we went. We were always fascinated going there.

Uncle Henry was a hunter so as a young child it sometimes was scary. He had moose heads with huge antlers hanging off his wall. On the other side hung a huge black bear that we later used for a rug. Uncle Henry's was magical. We would go fishing, boating, swimming, we even got to drive the speed boat once. As the years passed, my mother's friends began to get invited to come with us to forget the reality of life and that darkened the memory of Uncle Henry's quite a bit. Until then, it was a kid's dream to have what we had at Uncle Henry and Aunty Elma's house those plentiful summers and it gave me a taste of a life of freedom and happiness, the type of life all children should have.

Another event that turned into a blessing and changed my life was when my mom sent me to a Christian camp. For the first time in my life I belonged somewhere where people loved me. There were kids there that I could relate to. I was taught about Christianity and the gospel of Christ, and it made sense to me. That summer, the summer of 1994 I became a Christian. I accepted the gospel into my life and wanted to be different.

Every summer when camp rolled around I went to every opening possible, every time there was an open bed, I made sure I was in it. If I could go I went. It was amazing for me. At the end I cried. This meant I had to go back to Berkeley Street; back to where I was trying to run from. This meant back to be a slave, cleaning the house, doing laundry, cooking dinner. My sister and I did everything. If my mother wanted something all she needed to do was yell for us and we made sure to get there because we knew if we didn't do something fast enough or the way she wanted it to be done we got a smack or beating, whatever she had the energy for. She would call us names like stupid or bitch. I found that whatever I did was never fast enough or done the way she wanted it done, and I got used to the names and smacks .I got used to the beatings. It became normal for me.

I got smarter as I got older. I learned to duck faster and move quicker. Instead of waiting for a beating I ran away from her. I always thought that if it was possible to go to the bathroom for her I would have.

After camp my mother began to send me to church. I had a Sunday school teacher named Priscilla who taught me about love and the stories in the Bible. As a child it was a magical thing. When I got older I came to realize those stories are what formed the foundation of my belief in

Christianity. I began to learn how to do mime which is a form of dance. I sung in the children's choir. I did arts and crafts. I did Sunbeams, a program similar to Girl Scouts, in which I got badges for different things. For Christmas we would put on pageants and during the Easter season we would go to nursing homes and hand out gifts to the elderly. I had friends at church.

As I got older I started to learn about the Bible and the different ideas inside of the Bible like forgiveness, sin, prosperity, and love. I participated in every activity that I was allowed to. If it meant that I didn't have to be home I did it. Church began to be my safety place. I loved going there and being around the people that were there. They truly showed me love. For the first time in my life I felt wanted.

My mother seemed to never have the energy to take care of the house. She would say that is why God gave her children to be her slaves. I always remember this. But if it had to do with one of her "wonderful" boyfriends she was the first one moving; if it meant that she was going to feed her need for acceptance of her man she did it. She magically had the energy to do it for them.

Life had its ups and downs but for the first thirteen years of my life I didn't know which it was going to be for that day. It seems to me that I had more downs than ups. My mother loved her men and she never seem to choose the right kind of guys. She always seems to pick the bad guy type. Ones with serious records like pedophiles. She always made some kind of excuse for them so that the reality of the situation didn't seem that bad. She never seemed to care for the safety of her children. As long as she got what she wanted she picked them up.

Chapter 3

The Many Men

"Betray By Touch"
So young and innocent
This little girl plays
She doesn't even know she is in danger
She is alone with men much of the time
They play with her and tell her lies
She is young and innocent
They asked "Do you trust me"
She quivers and says yes
Why not her mommy trust them
She wouldn't dare put her in harm's way?
The clothes come off. Fingers start to roam in places that are private
Their clothes come off
Their kisses go all over her body
She is forced down to play the men's games
Force to touch parts that are hard
Ow! she screams in pain
SHH they say you said you trust me!
Tears roll down her face she wipes them away
This little girl only wanted to play so why did her mommy leave her to play with these men?
Pain, confusion roll in her head
sworn to secrecy
Out the door and she will soon find out that mommy sends her little innocent girl back to plan

*F*or as long as I could remember my mother always liked men that were violent or had some type of criminal record. As a young child I always had the feeling that I was not safe. I didn't know what safe felt like. I've already shown how my mother was unpredictable, however the men she surrounded herself with were even more unpredictable. Whoever she was "dating" automatically became our "daddy." She gave them complete control over discipline or anything else she didn't want to deal with. This was a problem since the majority of these men were either in jail or just out of jail. They were not good men.

More often than not, my punishments were less severe, especially when they were coming from one of my many daddy's. This was partly because I was the good one. My mother used to gloat about how good I was. I was the one she didn't have to stay on top of. It was also because her boyfriend's always took an interest in me. I was always their baby girl or their princess. They would hang my pictures in their jail cells. It wasn't until later in life that I came to understand why. As I said before, little girls can be so innocent. My mother would bring me to see these men in jail and had no problem putting me on their laps if they asked, allowing them to hold me and play with my hair in a seemingly innocent fashion.

On the days we went to the jail, she would talk about my daddy that we were going to see. Whoever the daddy of the month was at the time. Excitement was always in the air. It oozed out of her every pore and it was contagious. We would fill out the required paper work, take off our shoes and belts, empty everything out of our pockets, walk thru the metal detector and have a pat down. Every Saturday, Sundays and if we were real good sometimes during the week as well. As a young child I did not understand. As I grew older however, I became more aware of the many "Daddy's we had."

If I didn't go to the jail with my mother, I was left in the care of whoever was in the house who was old enough to babysit. Often, I was left with one of many aunts and uncles. It was one of these times that my first memory of sexual abuse occurred. It was when I was eight years old, however I think I may have been abused at a younger age. I can't remember for sure. I was in my sister's room, she was twelve at the time. Her boyfriend and boyfriend's brother were in the room, visiting. The door was closed and the lights were off. My sister and her boyfriend were on the bed and the brother who was sixteen grabbed me into a squatting position. As he did this he pulled down my pants and stuck his fingers inside me. I tensed up and jumped away. I pulled up my pants and swung open the door. My aunt and uncle were in the kitchen cooking, but I didn't say a word. I just ran to the bathroom and cried. When I pulled down my pants there was blood, so I changed my underwear.

My mother, as I said earlier, was not home. She was at a jail seeing my "step father," who also happened to be a level three sex offender! It was kind of ironic that she was not there to protect me because she was visiting him. This boy soon blabbed his mouth about what he had done. My mother confronted me about it and I told her it was true. She called the police; and I was interviewed. The boy was never tried because he was a minor. I heard that the people on the street who knew my family took care of him and I never saw him again. Life continued and my mother continued with the beatings.

I remember going to visit my stepfather in jail for the first time. His name was Kevin. He would talk with me. Give me hugs and kisses. He made my mother "happy," so everything was okay for a while. The day that he was getting released from jail, I looked at my mother and asked her if he hurt a girl. I'm not sure where I got the idea from, but I must have gotten it from somewhere.

She looked at me and said, "He did, yes. But she was 16 and she wanted him to have sex with him, so it was okay."

"Is he going to live with us?" I was worried that he might hurt me, even though he had never acted badly towards me when we visited him in jail. Something told me that something was wrong.

"Don't worry sweetie, everything is going to be all right. We are all going to be a family. You'll see."

He came home and at first it was okay. He did special things for me. At one point I got into a fight at school and he punished me at first but then unpunished me because I was protecting myself. But if my brother got into trouble it was a different story. He gave special attention to me.

He always wanted to have pillow fights with me. At first they were fun, but as we played pillow fight more, he began to tough and grab at my private body parts. He would pinch my butt. He would grab my breasts and twist them. He then began to grab at my vagina and try to insert fingers. My mother seemed to think it was funny. He was doing this to me and two other little girls in the neighborhood. She would sit there and laugh most of the time. I was the baby and men always seemed to want me, but that made no difference to Kevin. I was his, my own mother made sure of it.

We would watch movies together and play games together, as if we were a "family." One day my mother, Kevin and I were watching a movie. I was on top the comforter with Kevin, and my mother sat right by my side. She got up to do something, leaving me alone with him. Kevin seized the moment. He had become aroused. He grabbed my hand and placed it on his penis and started to have me jerk him off.

"No I don't want to," I said.

What he said next haunts me to this day. "All daddy's princesses do this for them."

I was scared. Kevin fell right back into drugs. He started to stay out late and hit my mother. One night I was awoken by yelling and screaming. My bedroom door was right across the hall from my mothers. Her eyes were black and blue and Kevin had her by her throat.

"I told you Dee not to fuck with me!"

"Stop!" I shouted.

He turned around and left and my mother told me to go back to bed.

No matter what happened, she always went back to him. She always fell for the 'I love you, I want to be with you, I won't do it again' act. She never learned, but I think she didn't want to learn. She always ran with people who did bad things. As long as she benefited from whatever she was chasing she continued on that path. She never grew up and her kids suffered for it.

Kevin was a registered sex offender and someone found out. It really was only a matter of time. There were fliers passed around and my mother couldn't hide it any longer. My friends from the neighborhood were not allowed to play with me at my house anymore.

One day before school my mother came in my room and sat on my bed.

"Kaelee, has Kevin ever touched you in a way you didn't like?" As if she didn't know. As I said before, she watched him play pillow fight with me and laughed as he did it.

"Yes, he has. Lots of times. He has also touched some of my friends too."

"Thanks for telling me, I'm going to fix it, okay? You don't have to worry anymore."

I went to the next door neighbor who Kevin had been molesting along with me, and told her that I told my mother. We went to school as usual, but we were soon pulled out of class and questioned by the guidance counselors. That night when I got home from school I was interviewed by some police officers. The case went to trial.

I was ten years old when I testified in Supreme Court against him while he sat there and watched me. It was a terrifying experience that no ten year old should have to go through. I knew what a courtroom was at ten. I was too young to really understand what was going on, but I was terrified. I was in therapy already, to help me deal with what was going on. To this day the layout of the court room is fresh in my mind.

When he lived with us, Kevin had originally worked at an electronics company where my aunt working was boss. I thought that things would get better once Kevin was gone. I was wrong. Once the truth had been told about Kevin, once he was gone, my life turned in a way that I never could have imagined.

Chapter 4

Manny

*K*evin went away. It was supposed to be better. It didn't last though, shortly after he was gone, in came Manny. At first everything was great. We had no idea. We thought he was just a friend of Kevin's from work coming by to help out. He told us that he was the same age as our mother, in his mid-forties. He was Spanish and spoke broken English. He really was in his sixties and his English was fine. He started to come around a little at first, helping out in small ways, but then the visits became more frequent. He and my mother were not dating, he was just a friendly neighbor who wanted to help out. Or so we thought.

It didn't take him long to figure out what my mother's needs and interests were. Who knows what Kevin had told him when they worked together. He figured out that as long as my mother had money there wasn't much that she would say no to. As long as her needs were met, it didn't matter what happened to her kids. He started to give her money for the bills and then he started buying food for the house. He gave her money to send to her boyfriends in jail and paid for our schooling supplies or field trips. He started to pay her bills. He was our Uncle Manny, and we loved to have him over. It was like every kids dream, our mom was happy, everyone was happy. Then the ultimate betrayal came.

Uncle Manny and my mother had a conversation about me and they came up with the Idea of having me give him English lessons because his English was so broken. He bought the material and showed it to my mother, offering to pay me $200.00 dollars every other week. All my mother saw was money. I guess the strangeness of the situation never occurred to her. Or it did and she just didn't care. Manny said I had to teach him the English lessons at his house across the street all by myself. My mother told me of the arrangement and that she had signed me up for the task. I was to begin teaching Manny his lessons at the end of my sixth grade in school. I was eleven years old.

I already told you about the first day with Manny. About what he did, how he followed me home to make sure I didn't tell. He made sure I stayed silent. I laid in my bed that night praying that what had happened to me would never happen again. But this was only the beginning of what would become my hell on Berkeley Street.

I didn't realize that the lessons were always going to run like the first lesson did. I was still in so much shock that it didn't register in my mind. Every day after school for three years I came home from school and across the street I went. Great old mom made sure that Uncle Manny had his lessons done each day because that meant that she was going to get paid. Then the summer started and the after school lessons turned into morning lessons, then they happened again in the afternoon.

Then Uncle Manny started to take me on errands with him. He was the one who taught me how to drive. He would put me on his lap and give me complete control over the vehicle while he focused on fingering me. We would drive on the back roads in a certain area where there wasn't a lot of traffic. He would unbutton my pants and force his fingers inside of me while I was driving. I would drive really fast hoping that he would stop. But it didn't really work, he continued to do it anyway. As he was teaching me how to drive he would pull down under a bridge during the day time and down by the river in the city and he would rape me there too. It began to seem to me that I was not safe anywhere I went.

Manny started to take the whole family out for dinners, nights at the beach, movie nights, anything that made it look like he was a wonderful man. Before every outing he needed an English lesson. My mother never questioned how many lessons that he needed. If I would protest she would get angry.

"Why don't you want to go over there?" She would smack me or punch me, "get over there you little bitch, you're so selfish!"

Off I went, realizing she wouldn't listen. She didn't want to. Mommy never protected me.

It got worse. Uncle Manny began to take me to work with him. He was a general contractor and he had a lot of empty houses and buildings that he worked at. He would take me to the houses and rape me during the day. Then he would also get his afternoon lesson at his house.

Eventually my mother allowed the ultimate betrayal, and Uncle Manny started sleeping in my bed at night. At first I didn't know what to do. I started to sleep on the outside of the bed so I was able to get away. He quickly figured that out and pushed me towards the wall as soon as he climbed into bed with me. Then I thought I got smart and I started to wear more clothes at night so that it would be harder for him to get at me. As if he would just give up if it got to be too much work. My nightly attire became underwear, bra, t-shirt nightgown, shorts, pajama pants, and a sweat shirt. He would get angry with me because I had so much clothing on but I continued to do it. He would hold me down and takeoff my clothes, layer by layer. I was awoken every night by the stripping of my clothes. I would try to yell for help, but he would cover my mouth and remind me that I trusted him. I would cry but no one ever came to my rescue.

I couldn't understand why my mother ignored my cries for help. My bed faced the door and it was always open. Her bed faced the door as well. "What did I do to deserve this?" I asked myself.

For a long time I believed that I was put on earth to fulfill this duty in life. It made my mother happy and I thought I could do this for her. As long as she was happy, my siblings and I didn't get any beatings. It was my sacrifice for my family. I was not being selfish any longer.

Uncle Manny started to control me in more and more ways. He put ideas in my head. He would tell me that no one could love me the way he loved me. I actually started to believe that he was the only one who could take care of me, that I had everything as long as I fulfilled my duty to him.

Manny was very jealous man. We would be driving in the car and he would yell at me for "looking at boys." He would say that I was looking at them as if I was taking their clothes off. I didn't even know what that meant or what he was talking about. He also broke up all my close relationships. I would go over to my friend's house and he would get angry and tell my mother lies about them so that I couldn't go any longer.

Manny controlled every aspect of my life. Everyone loved Uncle Manny. He knew my teachers and counselors at school because he got involved in so many activities. He volunteered to help with my church activities. He built stage props for the Christmas plays. He took me to my out of school counselor's appointments. He was the best thing that happened to my family and me, according to the people in my world. I felt trapped and very confused. I only trusted him, and yet I didn't trust him at all. My aunts would ask me all the time if something was happening and I always answered no. I was afraid of telling the truth. He would tell me that no one would believe me if I did tell because I let him do this to me and I believed him.

He would rape me but never ejaculate inside of me. He would always pull out before and let it come out on my belly. He then would take a towel or baby wipe and wash it off.

Uncle Manny came with us to Uncle Henry's for the summer in the year 2000. Uncle Henry's house was not that magical that year, Manny ruined it for me. He would send my mother to the store leaving Jeffery and I with him. Manny would tell me to go to the camper and get undressed because it was time for lessons. He would rape me and then we would get dressed and my mother would come back. At night my mother, Manny, Jeffery, and I would sleep in the camper. My mother slept at one end and Jeffery, Manny, and I would sleep on the other side. Again, Manny would need his lesson. My mother was right there in the same room and she did not protect her baby girl. Why did my own mother not roll over and save me? What did I do that she would allow a grown man take her baby and be destroyed? The whole time we were there it was the same routine every day, two to three times daily. Uncle Manny had his lessons and my mother totally ignored it. She ignored it and denied it until the day my brother admitted Manny had molested him too. Then, suddenly, she believed him.

Then came the day that I got my period. It's supposed to be an exciting time in a young girl's life. The day I became a woman. Manny somehow managed to taint that memory as well. We were on a field trip with school that day, and when we came back my stomach was upset so I went home early.

Even though I didn't feel well, I went across the street for Manny's lesson. I had to. As he pulled my pants down he discovered that I got my period. He proceeded with his lesson anyway. When he was done, he cleaned me up and told me not to say anything to anyone about my period. I went home across the street and changed and threw my underwear away. Uncle Manny went to the store to buy me pads. I told my sister that I had got my period, but she didn't believe me. She asked me if I was sure it was my period and I didn't poop?

"Are you sure you didn't poop your pants?"

I showed her my underwear and told her not to say anything. I was scared Uncle Manny would find out I told and get mad at me. In he came with the pads from the store. He took me and started to explain to me how to use a pad. Then the door opened and in walked my aunt and mother. My sister blabbed her mouth and everyone was excited. My aunt came into my room and saw Uncle Manny there. She slammed the door open.

"What the fuck do you think you're doing? Get out of this room right now!"

Then she took me to the bathroom and showed me how to use a pad. I finally became a woman.

Manny continued to rape me several times a day for another year. I'm lucky I never got pregnant. Towards the end of eighth grade Uncle Manny stopped coming after me as much. One of the last times I had an after school lesson with him was for my eighth grade banquet, because I needed a new dress. But the lessons had become much less frequent. The last day Uncle Manny had his afternoon lesson was on June 3, 2000.

Then I found out he molested my cousin who was five years younger than I was. I confronted him on it and he told me to mind my business. I got very upset and decided that she would not suffer the way I did. I would find a way for him to stop.

The summer before I entered high school, I went to summer camp as usual. I had become close with a camp counselor named Stacey a few years before. I loved Stacey very much. She came back year after year and we always had some sort of run in. I loved her and I trusted her. That summer, I told her that I needed to talk to her. That it was important. I had decided to break the silence. I knew that it was the only way to save my cousin. I didn't care that I was being abused but I refused to let her to go through what I had been through.

I remember it was a Sunday morning because we were at church in the shell at camp. There was an altar call and I went forward, begging God for it all to stop and then I grabbed Stacey. She must have realized it was important because she hugged me and brought me out of church to the side of the shell. I broke down between two little trees on the grass and told Stacey that I was being sexually abused.

Stacey cried with me. "Kaelee," she held my hand and looked me in the eyes. "Did you want him to do those things to you?"

"No."

"You know that what he did was wrong, right? It's not your fault that he did that to you."

She took a deep breath and looked away for a second, thinking. Then she gave me a big hug. "Everything is going to be okay now," she said. "I promise."

Then I started crying even more while she prayed with me.

Everything in my life was different from that day forward. I was interviewed by the camp director and Mrs. Smith, the pastor's wife. I was then interviewed by a child protective services worker. They told me that I would not be returning home and that I would be going to my pastor's house to stay with them temporarily until they figured out what to do next. I was so afraid but also relieved because at least I knew who I was going to live with. I found out my twin was

One of the things my foster parents did that was new to me was they worked as a team. When I was nasty with my foster mom, my foster dad got mad at me as well. I never had two parents who parented at the same time before and at first I didn't understand why my foster dad got upset. He would say, "If you are mad at my wife you are mad at me, because we work as a team." This upset me and I didn't know how to handle it so I would cut even more.

I craved so hard to be a part of a family, and I never really felt as though they saw me that way. As I said before, they told me I couldn't call them mom and dad. When we went places as a family they would introduce the family as "these are our sons and this is our foster daughter". I always felt like an outsider, like I didn't belong to anyone. They fed me and clothed me, and made sure my basic needs were taken care of, but more often than not I felt like a check. It hurt for a long time.

Entering high school is always a big transition for any child. But it was an even bigger one for me. On the first day, Mrs. and Mr. Smith brought me and changed the paper work into their names, and then just left me. It was all so overwhelming and I didn't know what to do.

Before all of this happened, I had a friend named Deidra. Deidra had a lot of problems. One of her problems was drugs, and I was interested in that side of her, but Uncle Manny put a stop to that before it became a problem for me as well. One thing I am grateful for. But Deidra did show me a technique that would help me to cope with all of the changes in my life. It was in the eighth grade, right in the middle of science class. She took a pin and cut herself in class and showed it to me. That was it I was addicted. My life was forever changed.

Even though I was no longer at my mother's house getting raped by Uncle Manny, the cutting continued. One day Mrs. Smith picked me up from school to bring me to the court house to give my story to court. On the drive down, she confronted me on it.

"Kaelee are you cutting yourself?"

She looked at me before turning her attention back to the road. I tried to change the subject.

"Kaelee, I'm going to ask you again, are you cutting yourself?"

I didn't say anything for a minute. I didn't know what to say. Finally I gathered up the courage to tell her.

"Yes," I said. "I am. What are you going to do about it?"

"I have to tell your case worker. She will know what to do."

I shrugged. I didn't care. My body was mine and I was going to do whatever I wanted to it. No one was going to do or say anything different that was going to stop me from doing it. It was the only thing that made me feel okay.

At the court house I met with two gentlemen who took my story about Manny and what he put me through. I answered so many questions about the abuse, but I remember leaving the court not feeling like I told them everything. I didn't tell them everything. They shouldn't have had men questioning me, it made me uncomfortable and it was hard to answer all of their questions properly.

"What was I to do?" I thought. "Would they really believe me if I told them everything?"

There was so much going on, I still don't know if I fully understood what was happening. In fact, the case ended up getting dropped because his lawyer caught me off guard with a question that I hadn't covered in the interview. Since I provided conflicting information, they claimed I was lying.

Everything was happening so fast and now I had to worry about hiding my cutting addiction on top of it. My mind was spinning.

We went home that night and my foster parents sat me down. They asked me what I was cutting with and I showed them my safety pin. They confiscated it like that would stop me. They told me it had to stop. It didn't.

I started to use whatever I could get my hands on. I was using safety pins, earrings, paper clips, pins, knives, razors, it didn't matter to me. As long as I was cutting I was in control. This was the one thing that no one had any control over except me. My foster mom started to check me. She would check my wrists because that was where I was cutting at the time. I got smart and started moving up my arms, then my legs, then my belly, chest, pelvis, ankles; everywhere. She would strip me naked looking for new spots thinking if she was checking me I would not cut, but this only perpetuated the cutting further. It was like a game to try and figure out where I can go next. I was sad to see the disappointment on her face when she found out the new places and I even stopped for a little while to make her happy. But I couldn't keep it up and I went back to it. She stopped looking after a while.

Cutting gave me power. No one could take it away. I did it for a variety of reasons. It felt good to watch myself bleed. Then it became a rush of energy, a soft of high that I got from it. It became a game to see who I could hide it from. I felt like no one cared so I didn't care either. My life at the time was full of so much change and it was a constant. My mother was a bitch. She couldn't take care of me, and she never even tried. I was put into foster care, separated from my family. I had so many reasons to cut.

My first year of high school was tough but I got through it. I attended a vocational high school and wanted to go into their nursing program. In order to get into the program as a freshmen you had to go through a week of introduction of the program and you rotate out throughout the programs the school provides. Then you pick your top three programs that you are interested in.

When I first went through my rotation of the program they denied me. They assumed I would be like my sister and just cause trouble. I was so upset I went to the guidance office and demanded to be given another chance. I was successful and was placed back in the program. They were shocked at how different my sister and I were. I have always been different from my siblings. I was the "smart" one. I was the attractive one. I was the one that excelled at everything that I did. Everyone loved me. That ran true for my foster parents as well.

They had the opportunity to take my brother in as well and declined. I understood why. My brother had a lot of problems with behavior and respect. I understood, but secretly I wanted him with me. I couldn't imagine being pulled from home, put into a stranger's house and told not to go home, like he was. I felt sorry for him and lucky to be where I was at. I also felt bad because I knew my twin was angry. We were supposed to be together but we were not, two different houses, two different sets of parents. There was nothing I could do.

Freshman year had its bumps and bruises although I got through it. Being in a foster home was supposed to be temporary but it seemed to get longer and longer. I would have family meetings at department of social services. My mother, sister, brother, and aunt would go. One day we were visiting and a fight broke out. My brother ended up punching a hole through the wall, my mother ended up crying and I ran away wanting to go back home to my foster family. They came and got me and I told them that I didn't want to go back. I didn't want to see them anymore and they said I didn't have to. It was finished. That was when things started to change and my foster family started to accept me a little more.

Originally, I was only supposed to live with my foster parents for three months while my mother got her act together and then I was supposed to go home, but that never happened. The holidays came and I remember my foster mother looking at me and pointing her finger in my face, saying, "You are coming with us for Christmas, don't ruin our holidays with your attitude." I felt so hurt. I was away from my family for the first time in my life for the holidays and yet didn't feel happy.

We went home to Pennsylvania for Christmas. That is where my foster mom's family is from. The family accepted me, in spite of my foster mom's concerns. They were all so welcoming and willing to take me in. I had a good time. I called my mother and sister and it was a good day. We stayed on vacation and I met more of my foster mom's family.

My foster mom has a cousin Rachel who is special needs and she took right to me. She has had many surgeries throughout her life. She is a very sick person and yet she has the spirit of an angel. Everyone loves her so much, especially my foster brothers Chris and Tommy. She is so funny. Rachel will always be special to me. Rachel helped me to feel more accepted in my foster family. She was and still is a cousin to me.

When my foster dad's side of the family came over for family gatherings, my foster parents were awesome. Everyone wanted details and you could tell they were curious and felt sorry for me. Whenever that happened, my foster parents kept me close and didn't explain anything. It was just as it was and no questions, no answers. Those were the first times I felt like I belonged, like I was theirs.

Sophomore year was very challenging for me academically. I had the two worst teachers in the school. My geometry teacher didn't know how to discipline people who didn't want to learn. I tried to do my work, but the chaos in the classroom and the lack of control made it difficult for me to learn the lessons. My English teacher was very tough but in a different way, we had ten to fifteen page papers due on a regular basis and he was very strict with the students. These two teachers made school hard on me during that year.

I recommitted being Christian in my sophomore year or at least I thought I did. I used to tell my friends all about God and they always came to me with their problems. I was a good listener, and good at giving advice. I never threw it on them but they knew I was different because I believed. They would ask me to pray for things for them and I did.

Suddenly, I had a very busy home life. Since my foster parents were Ministers, we had a church to run. There was always some kind of program running that I needed to help with. I helped run the children's ministry on Monday and Friday. There was a prayer meeting on Tuesday. Wednesday was family night with my foster family. Thursday was sometimes at home but usually not, we almost always had a Bible study or similar event going on. Friday I had youth group after the children's ministry. Saturday we had music programs and of course Sunday was church. I taught Sunday school and helped out with the services all day. Then there were always extra programs going on, depending on the season.

Christmas was huge. We had Christmas plays, I rang bells to collect money for the church, we had an Angel tree where people would buy Christmas presents for needy families and we would distribute them. In the spring we would visit nursing homes and distribute gifts to the elderly. We would have kids from the church help us out. On top of all of that my parents ran a food pantry plus the usual church duties that kept them, and the rest of us busy during the days. I never had time for friends outside of school.

In the summer I worked at the camp I went to as a child, camp Wonderland, where we would bus kids in from the inner cities and give them a week of Christian based camping. I had trained for two weeks as an S.I.T. (staff in training) the year I told Stacey about Manny. I worked for two weeks and learned the jobs I could do at the camp. After that I was guaranteed a position for the following summer and every year thereafter.

My foster parents expected me to be a shining example of what a child of pastors should be. I was not allowed more than ten minutes on the phone with friends from school, so my friends did not call me. It was hard. I went from being a nobody in an abusive house to a somebody in a Christian family. I had responsibilities that I never had before. I had people looking at me from every direction. I felt like I couldn't do anything wrong because I had so many eyes on me. I used to get mad at my foster parents because they would say I was so disrespectful, but looking back, I was. But at the time I couldn't understand their point of view. I felt that I had no room to breathe. My friends were out having fun and I was stuck doing church stuff all the time.

Not that I didn't enjoy it. But it was hard to adjust. I went from being prostituted to my neighbor to being the pastor's daughter. I was trying so hard to fit in, but I really just became bossy. I was always telling everyone what they could and couldn't do because I felt that was what I was supposed to be doing. It was invigorating, but stressful because I wasn't really in the right frame of mind for it.

My birth family stopped calling and I didn't hear from them anymore. During the summer between my sophomore and junior year of high school my foster parents applied for and received legal guardianship over me. I remember being at home with my foster mom shortly after that. She was making a salad and I was standing at the kitchen counter and I accidentally called her mom. We both stopped what we were doing for a second and she looked at me.

"I'm sorry…" I stuttered. "I know you said to call you Mrs. Smith, but now you're sort of my mom, right?" She didn't say anything. "Is it okay? Can I call you mom?"

She took a deep breath, as if it was something she had expected but wasn't prepared to answer. And then, the answer I had been dreaming of. "Yes Kaelee, you can call me Mom."

Dad soon followed. Finally I had my dream family.

My 16th b-day was incredible. I was taken to my first concert with a group of friends. It was to my favorite band at the time Creed. My first time to a concert. I was a bit naïve. I said to John, who was the youth pastor and my friend Karen's brother, "Look at the balloons. He said, "Kay that not a balloon!" I felt so embarrassed.

My friend Karen took me to get my ears pierced. While we were there, I started talking to her about my parents.

"Wouldn't it be crazy if they actually threw me a sweet sixteen?" I said. I didn't actually think they would, I was joking around.

Karen kind of looked away for a second. "Yeah right, Kaelee, you know your parents better than that."

The way she said it was a little awkward though, almost forced. Then Karen kept getting calls while we were out. Suddenly my brain was going a hundred miles an hour. What if they were throwing me a sweet sixteen? Could I possibly hope for something as incredible as that? I tried not to get my hopes up too much, I didn't want to be disappointed.

We drove home and as soon as we turned onto the circle where we lived, my hopes and dreams were fulfilled. They actually threw me a surprise sweet sixteen. I was honored and so grateful. I was given over $800 dollars in gift money. I used it towards my first car.

So many things changed that day. I had the world in my hands. I had the family of my dreams. Everything in my life was just perfect. I couldn't have been happier. God was my friend, he gave me the family of my dreams. I couldn't imagine being without them in my life.

Chapter 6

Chaos

Things got better for a while after that. I stopped cutting for almost two years because I didn't feel like I needed to any more. I excelled in so many things in my life during that time. Unfortunately, it was only temporary as I still had so much going on in the background that I hadn't really dealt with.

I had an awesome counselor at the time, named Beth. She told me that I had PTSD which I didn't understand at the time. We talked a lot about my behavior at home and most of all cutting. I had stopped, but I still had urges. She felt that I was depressed and I definitely was. I just didn't show it to others. My sessions with Beth were the only place that I could feel. I could be sad, or angry, or have irrational thinking. I could say anything and she didn't judge me. She would take walks with me or sit with me, whatever I needed. She was just willing to listen. I loved her so much. Beth felt that I was really depressed and wanted me to take an antidepressant. I didn't want to take it for a long time but I eventually agreed with it.

One reason I fought it was because my mom didn't feel that I needed medication. She came to the appointment and I was placed on an antidepressant. The second appointment we got into a fight and she refused to go to the appointment with me. Beth told her that she needed her to come into the appointment because I was still a minor. She did and as time went on she noticed a change in me.

I graduated high school at the top of my class. I received two plaques with my name on them for being the top of my shop. I received eleven scholarship offers from my high school that I could use towards any college I wanted. One of these scholarships was due to the great relationship I had with my mentor, Linda Cote. She was a major part of the nursing program at school and she took me under her wing and supported me throughout high school. I could come to her with anything and she knew most of what was going on in my life. She made a huge difference in my life.

My SAT scores were low though, so I attended a local community college. My first year there, I started to have adult relationships. I wanted to feel good about sex, I wanted to cover up the anger and the pain with positive experiences. I knew that I was a woman who could seduce men if I wanted and I set out to do it because now I was an adult and there were no longer legal constraints. It was also a control thing, and a way to rebel against my foster parent's attempts to keep me a child longer than I wanted. These relationships ended up causing problems for me in a number of ways. The first one was with Jonathan.

Jonathan was my childhood sweetheart. We went to the same church and high school. We did everything together. We dated our sophomore year of high school, but then he decided to date some other girl in my shop because she was allowed a lot more freedom than I was. In spite of that, we went to both proms together. We did all the same church activities together. We were inseparable. We started dating again the same day we graduated; June 9, 2004. I was very aggressive with him sexually. I wanted to have sex and I didn't care when or how, I just wanted it. We fooled around more than he wanted to, and he ended up breaking up with me because he didn't want to disrespect my parents. It was a very noble thing he did but I didn't see it that way at the time. I would end up searching him out when I got older, he was and always will be my first love.

After things ended with Jonathan, I started to go after my youth group leader. He was eight years older, and in many ways he practically helped raise me. I loved him very much. I also knew that I would be able to seduce him. On our first date I wore tight, low-rise jeans and black tank top with a sheer shirt over it. I was out to get one thing and I didn't care how I got it. We fooled around and I ended up telling him in the heat of the moment that I loved him. We started having sex that night and sneaking around behind my parents and my foster sister's back. We would find any excuses we could to go out together. Our 'dates' turned into sex sessions.

School was very stressful for me at the time as well. I was a full time college student and also working as a certified nursing assistant at the hospital on a very stressful floor. It was made worse by the sneaking around and the guilt I felt because of my Christian background. My foster dad kept on asking me if I was having sex and I kept lying to him which only made things worse. I felt like I was living a double life and eventually I could not handle it anymore and I broke up with my youth group leader. After we broke up, both my parents confronted me about their suspicion that we were having sex. That was when I finally admitted it to them, yes I was having sex. I didn't tell them I ended it with him because of the guilt I felt, but I think they knew. They knew but they didn't want to admit it. They were devastated.

I began to break down with feelings of guilt and I had no one to turn to. Beth had left me for a new job when high school ended and I started college with a new counselor. My new counselor was pregnant and she would be leaving for maternity leave, so I didn't really talk to her, because it seemed pointless. I was depressed and suicidal and I needed a good counselor at the time and I just didn't have one.

When she left for maternity leave, they placed me with Sarah for three months. Sarah was gay and at first she was apprehensive about being my therapist because of my religious parents. I looked her in the face and told her that I did not care what my parents thought, I needed help and she was going to be the one to help me. That was all I cared about. She said ok, that she would keep me as a client. She told the counselor who was waiting to transfer me that she was going to keep me. She started to tell me that I need a break from my life and I should consider going on a little vacation. Sarah and Beth were close friends and she had spoken to her about me and those conversations combined with my chart had led her to that conclusion. I told her she was crazy and I was not crazy. I was not going anywhere.

My parents were beside themselves as to finding out that I was having sex. I think they were so embarrassed by the choices that I made for myself that they wanted to hide me away. They felt that they needed to discipline me. One Tuesday night I went to my night class then headed to the church for youth programs.

I was in the office getting ready to go downstairs to be with the kids when my dad told two younger teens to go downstairs to be with the kids.

"If they go with the kids, what am I supposed to do?" I asked him.

He looked at me coldly. "Nothing I don't even know why you're here."

I got the message loud and clear. I picked up my bag and left the church.

After leaving the church that night, I called my mentor from high school Linda Cote. Linda was also a nurse and advised me to go see Sarah. I went to her office where she was waiting for me after hours with her supervisor. They took my car keys and decided that I needed to be assessed by the crisis team at the hospital.

Sarah had to convince my parents to leave my brothers' soccer game so they could come to her office and pick me up and bring me to the hospital. When they arrived, they were not happy. They were mad at me for disrupting their night, and even unhappier with Sarah because they didn't like her very much. There was no conversation in the car as we drove to the hospital.

We walked into the emergency room and they took me right in because of my age. Anyone under a certain age is a priority for psych emergency room visits. I remember undressing. I was put on a gurney and my parents stood by my side but when I went to reach for my mom, she backed up.

"No, Kaelee. I'm so angry with you right now, please don't touch me."

This made me really pissed off. I needed them and they didn't want to help me, they couldn't even see what was going on. All they cared about was missing the boys' soccer game.

I talked to the crisis worker and then she talked to my parents. She decided that I was a candidate for inpatient on the hospital's psych ward based on what we had told her. My parents told me they loved me, and then they just left. I felt so abandoned and upset, I cut myself while I was in the emergency room. The crises worker put me on suicide watch. Eventually I was brought upstairs to the psych floor and they kept me on a one to one, where someone follows you and watches you everywhere you go, for the first few days. They put me on antidepressants and in two weeks I went home.

When I got back home, nothing was different. The antidepressants didn't help. I was still suicidal, and I was cutting again. I never felt as alone in my life as I did at that time. In spite of this, I jumped right back into the same routine; school, church, and work. Three months later I swallowed half of a bottle of Advil, 50 pills at 200 mg each, then I took my antidepressants on top of that. My mom called me the next morning and woke me up. It didn't work, I was still alive and I was pissed.

"Ugh, mom? What the hell?"

"Kaelee? Are you still asleep?" she asked. "Get up. I need you to come help out with passing gifts to the elderly in nursing homes."

"I can't do that right now, I can't drive."

"You can't drive? Why can't you drive? Kaelee, that's crazy."

"I overdosed, Mom."

"What? You better get to the hospital right now! Your father and I are coming home to take you to the hospital right now. Don't you dare go anywhere!" She hung up the phone and I just stared at it wondering where she thought I would go.

It was Easter, and no one came to see me at the hospital. It was so awful. After that I lost a part of me, even more than what I felt before. My foster family was not prepared to handle my mental issues and no matter how much I wanted them to, they couldn't accept the seriousness of it. I needed them to be my family, but that meant I needed them to support me and they just couldn't do that.

Chapter 7

New Beginning

I had been accepted to Messiah College for the nursing program. It was a GOD send as I thought because I was finally going to have a chance to get out on my own and have some freedom. I was also going to be going to school for what I really wanted to do. It was exactly what I wanted.

That summer I worked at our Salvation Army Camp Wonderland as the canteen queen. The canteen queen was in charge of the camp store. It was a fun job because the shifts were short and I had a lot of freedom to get involved in other areas of the camp. That was my last year at camp and I felt more involved that year than ever before. Camp was always wonderful. It was where I was first saved when I was eight. I had made so many lifelong friends there. Each year we looked forward to seeing each other again the following year, and as we got older we would write letters back and forth. Then we started to meet up at divisional outings where all the Salvation Army youth would get together and do some kind of group activity. We had youth praise, where we would meet and have a worship service together; "See you at the Pole," where we met at a flag pole in the fall to pray together as a group; and youth counsel every May. It was epic, whenever we got together we picked up right where we left off the year before. GOD was truly among us.

The year I started college, I drove seven and a half hour down to Grantham, Pennsylvania after camp was over. I was a bit overwhelmed when my parents and I walked the grounds the first time and I realized that I was staying behind. My brothers were too young to understand what was going on, they didn't realize that I was leaving. Messiah College was a Christian College and they had a beautiful candle light service to welcome us to campus. After that, my parents helped me unpack. I remember they were going through my clothes and deciding what I needed and didn't need. It was quite humorous, especially when my dad got rid of all my thongs. My mom was crying as they left, showing that she was actually going to miss me. I will always treasure that memory.

They were gone and I was left to fend for myself. It was my first time away from home and in so many ways I felt so isolated. I couldn't just get in my car and go home for the weekend. I had to make wise decisions as to who I was as a person. I prayed and went to church on Sundays and even did Bible studies. My roommates Brittany and Amber were awesome. They showed me the ropes and were supportive of me when I was so far from home and struggling. They were both from the area so they often went home on the weekends, though, and they didn't really understand how hard it was to be alone all weekend. I was little jealous but more than that, I was lonely.

One weekend, I went to a party where I met a boy named David, from DC. I gave him my number and he called me that night. I was in heaven. David loved the Lord and was still a virgin. I was impressed by his enthusiasm for the Lord. I was always smiling and happy when he was around. I don't remember our first date but I do remember him walking me to the door and kissing me. After that, we spent every moment together. My mom was always on my back about how much time I was spending with David. Whenever they called we were together. I slacked on my studies, which I couldn't really afford to do. Finals came and I realized that I didn't make the grades to stay in the nursing program. I had to choose another major or drop out. I chose to drop out and David and my friends helped me pack my things into my car and on I went to Somerset, Massachusetts where my parents had moved the family a few months before I went to Messiah college. I wish I hadn't done that, it was definitely a big mistake.

When I first moved back home, everything was good. Part of the deal for moving back home was that I had to find a new therapist. Her name was Elizabeth. I thought I was going to like her, but she wasn't attentive enough and caused problems for me.

Then I began to have thoughts about killing my family and I started to have auditory hallucinations telling me to hurt my family. I agonized for weeks with it in secret. One day I was working in the emergency room and I was sent to a supply closet to get something. I saw it a scalpel and I impulsively took it, thinking I now had the weapon I wanted to use to kill my family. I had seen it used for many procedures and knew how sharp it was, and in the moment it felt like the right decision.

I knew deep down that something in my spirit was off, that these thoughts were wrong and that I needed help. I didn't know how to go about telling my secret though. How do you tell someone that you fantasize about killing the people you love? I tried to tell my therapist by writing her a letter. But I didn't feel right just saying it, so I talked about other things first. My letter started off talking about how I was disgusted with my body. I said that I thought I was fat even though I only was barely 100 lbs. In hindsight, it was a tactic of mine to avoid the real issue. At the bottom of the letter I described my sick fantasy in just a few sentences, but my therapist was so caught up in the issue of physical beauty that I presented first that she never even got to that part. My cry for help went unnoticed. The next thing I did was to confide in someone that I knew would get me help.

My parents ran a home for teenage mothers and their babies. They had an employee Mrs. D who was a social worker. I told her I had something important to tell her and she invited me to her house. I sat down with her and told her everything. I told her that I had been hearing voices that were telling me to kill my parents. She said that she was concerned and that she would get back to me about it. I left Mrs. D's. house feeling relieved at first. Then I had a rush of adrenaline kick in because my deep dark secret was out in the universe and I could never take back what I said. I went to bed that night scared about what was going to happen next, but knowing that there was no longer anything I could do about it.

The next morning I woke up as my brothers were going to school and I jumped in the shower, got out and waited. My phone began to ring. It was my mom calling me from work.

"Hello?"

Silence.

"Mom? Are you okay?"

"Kaelee, why?"

This time I was the one who was silent.

"I'm not just worried about us, I'm really worried about you Kaelee. This isn't normal."

"I'm sorry mom. I don't know what to do or where to go. I've been trying to tell someone for a while now."

"You need to call Elizabeth." She said and then hung up the phone.

I didn't know it at the time, but Mrs. D had already contacted my therapist through a friend on the board where I went to counseling. Right after my mom hung up the phone, Elizabeth called.

"Kaelee? Is it true?"

"Is what true?" I knew what she was talking about but I wanted to make sure.

"Why didn't you tell me? Why did you have to go to someone else?"

"I did tell you. It was in the letter I wrote you, but you never finished reading it."

She sighed. "Kaelee, you need to come into the office. Now. If you don't we are going to have to call the police."

I gathered my things and drove to the office. The whole time I was going over what they were going to do to me, wondering what was going to happen. When I got there I saw the psychiatrist. She changed my medication and then let me leave.

I was flabbergasted! I couldn't believe they just let me leave. I told them I heard voices telling me to kill my family and I even took a weapon home; that I had the whole thing planned out and they just let me leave. I didn't know what to do. My cry for help had been unanswered and I didn't trust myself to go back home.

I went to the beach and climbed up on the lifeguard chair and began to self-destruct. I started to cut my arms and wrists with the scalpel I had stolen. I cut my whole forearm on both arms to shreds. But it didn't do anything for me. It just made me angrier. I sat there crying, not sure of what to do or where to go.

I was there all day. At some point, my parents called me and told me to meet them at the D's house to hear out my options. They sounded worried and I expected them to tell me that I had to go to the hospital again. I met them there at 9pm.

I was not prepared for what happened next. My parents told me that I needed to get my belongings and move out of their house! My dad told me to go back to my birth family! I couldn't believe it! What a smack in the face. It stung me for a long time, years later I still replay that scene in my head over and over. I was upset, but it showed up as anger. With a rush of adrenaline and an "I'll show you" attitude, I went down to the house and threw as much as I could of my belongings into my car and I left. The D's had made a call to a Sister who ran a house for women with low income. Since I didn't have any other options, I drove to Fall River, Massachusetts where the house was. I was so frustrated and could not believe that my life was doing this to me at the moment.

Thrown Away

You said that you loved me.
You said that you wanted me to be a part of your family
You said that you would stand by me no matter the obstacles
Then how come it was so easy for you to throw me away?
You said that God loves me no matter the sin, sickness, or decision that I make
He is always there
Then why as my pastors more yet my parents that is was so easy for you to throw me away
You have been chosen to be the reflection of God and yet you live a lie because
GOD has not thrown me away!!!!

I knocked on the door and a few ladies answered. I asked for Sister Claire. I went up a flight of stairs to her room, but she was not there. I was so angry. "Maybe she croaked," I said.

Then she came around the corner and introduced herself. She had been there the whole time, she had just gone up a different flight of stairs. Then she explained the rules of the house. She told me how much it cost to stay there and I wrote her a check. The girls then proceeded to ask me if I wanted help bringing up my belongings and I said no. I showed Sister Claire my arms, in some desperation that someone would do something. I knew I needed to go to the hospital and wanted someone to send me there and no one would do it. When I showed Sister Claire my arms, she said, "Oh, that must be painful." But she still didn't do anything. The girls then asked again and I snapped back this time, angrier than ever. "NO!" I did it all myself. I don't know how many trips I made to the third floor that night but when I was finished I laid on the bed and cried myself to sleep.

Chapter 8

Getting Help

The following day I woke up and realized that I needed the kind of help that none of the people I confided in could give me. I packed a bag and went over to the crisis center. As I walked in I began to cry. I was out of my mind talking like a robot. I told the crisis team what had happened the day before and about my plan to kill my parents. I told them about the voices and my living situation. They asked me if I still had the scalpel I told them yes. They asked me to give it to them, and I did so with a sense of relief. It felt like my ordeal was finally coming to a close, I was finally going to get some help and then everything could return to normal. Unfortunately I was wrong, my pain was just beginning.

Pain is......

Pain is waking up the next morning and asking yourself what the fuck just happen

Pain is when you walk into a crises center and being completely out of your mind

Pain is when you talk to a stranger and the send you to the ER for a med clearance just to send you to a psyche ward to stabilize you

Pain is when you sleep for days and don't care if you live or die

Pain is when you hear from your dad that you're not allowed home because there is a restraining order against you

Pain is when b-days and holidays come and you're left to fend for your self

Pain is when you're in the same state and you can't even go visit

Pain is when you hear your brothers in the back ground and you can't talk to them

Pain is when you cry and all you want to do is to run home to your mom for her to hold you and tell you that things are going to be ok

Pain is when you are driving in the car and all you can think of is to smash your care into a tree

Pain is when you see your friends and their family together and they say that they understand
how can they?
Pain is when you wake up in the morning in a room with the only thing you have is pictures
Pain is when you can't sleep at night because all you can think about is hurting yourself and others
Pain is when you have to say good bye to one of the biggest supports in your life and move on
Pain knows that you have to start all over and learn to trust someone else with your deepest
secrets in your life
Pain is being afraid of yourself because you don't know what you are capable of
Pain is being scared to death about what you are thinking and what you might do....

The emergency room sent me to High Point Treatment Center in Plymouth, MA. The center was small, there was only one corridor with rooms off to the side. There was one activity/music room and a dining hall that was used as the TV room as well. There was a quiet room right at the beginning of the hallway near the nurse's desk. I was checking the whole place out to identify areas I could go for peace and quiet. When I got there, I slept for hours not getting up to eat or anything. I hardly made it to the bathroom. The only time I ever got up was when the staff came to get me to meet with the psychiatrist. I remember weighing 98 pounds when I entered the hospital.

They began to medicate me. They put me of high doses of several different kinds of tranquillizers including Depakote, Risperidone, Ativan, and Wellbutrin. I remember these ones in particular because of the side effects. Depakote in particular made me hungry. I ate so much and I gained like 30 pounds in the month that I was there. I was totally mortified.

I began to grow relationships with the staff. One person who I became particularly close to was Charlene. She was an older person, and had been around the block a few times which ended up being helpful for me. She took notice in me because we lived in the same town, Fall River, MA. One day I was having a hard time and Charlene took me by the hand and brought me to the side. She was trying to talk to me to calm me down when I began to vomit. I was having a flashback and was out of control. She took me outside to a caged in area where they took people out to smoke, hoping to help calm me down, but I threw myself to the ground and started to punch the cement instead. I was totally out of control.

The Restraint

I am very upset and I am talking to an aide
I can't hear her and I can't seem to get it together
I fall against a fence and start to punch concrete to make it stop
The next thing I know I am being picked up from the ground by men and women
She takes me outside to calm me down
I am shaking
I am yelling for it to stop
I begin to vomit
And I do not know what's going on

It does not seem to matter to me at the moment because all I can hear is someone screaming
Then I realize that it is me and I can't stop it
The next thing I know they put me on a hard bed and tie my arms and legs to the bed
I jump up and a person slams me back on the bed with their hand
The aide is at my head rubbing her hand on my forehead telling me that it's going to be alright
I can hear the nurse ask the doctor if he wanted her to give me something to calm down
The doctor stands dumb founded as to what to do
The aide is still telling me that it's going to be ok and I'm starting to calm down
I lay there motionless because I can't figure out what to do
I cry…..

I knew from that day forward that this would never happen to me again. I would never let myself get to the point where I had to be restrained again and I didn't. I never felt so out of control before in my life. But this was just the beginning of the long journey in front of me. I stayed at High Point for 30 days. The doctors and staff didn't want me to leave because they felt I was still unstable, but my insurance was kicking me out and they didn't have much say in the matter. The hospital gave me prescriptions I was to fill and take and a number to a day program they suggested I go to. I left there feeling so overwhelmed with life and unsure if I was ready to face reality. The cab ride from the hospital was very long and it didn't end at home. I wasn't welcome there anymore. I had made arrangements to stay with Sister Claire. I got there, paid my rent, and went to my room. I remember feeling fat because none of my clothes fit. I no longer fit in my clothes, I no longer fit in my skin, and I now had to relearn how to live life before I was really ready.

As I was rummaging through my things I came across the number I was supposed to call when I got home. It was for a place called Pathways in Taunton, Massachusetts. It was a trip from where I was staying, but I was determined to get better no matter what I had to do. They were expecting my call and I spoke to the intake therapist and set up an appointment for the next day. As I was driving there I made up my mind. I was going to do whatever it took to get my family back. I was willing to do anything. I walked into Pathways however and my resolve wavered some. Maybe this wasn't the best place for me, I thought. I'm not as bad as these people. This is an adult day-care really, they can't help me. But then I remembered my family and I knew I had to at least try. I didn't realize it at that moment, but I really was just like these people in every aspect.

I met with the team and learned about the program. One thing that I was expected to do was attend DBT; dialectical behavioral therapy taught by Marsha Lineham. DPT was designed to help people who had borderline personality disorder (BPD) like me. I thought if this is going to help "cure" me then I'll try it. I went to Pathways for four months, five days a week from 9-230pm, which provided me with a lot of structure and was very helpful. I worked weekends at the hospital and was able to maintain my part time basis while I got help and still pay my bills.

My therapist at Pathways was Beth, she specialized in DBT. When I found out, I felt comforted at first because her name reminded me of my old therapist from when I was a teenager. The similarity ended there and it was not the same kind of relationship. Beth was tough and that was what I needed at the time.

I was suicidal for most of the time I was at Pathways and the staff knew it. Whenever I got into my stuff I became suicidal and I was hospitalized more times than I care to remember. I would get suicidal and Beth would say let me get Sharon's opinion. Sharon was the supervisor at Pathways and she was tough too. Every time Beth went to get her I would know another ride to the emergency room was coming.

It was a revolving door for me, I was hospitalized at least every other month. They were long stays, however because I would max out the number of days allotted for a person on the Masshealth insurance plan. Then I was out the door and back to the day program, whether the doctors felt I was ready for it or not.

Chapter 9

The New Family

In the midst of going in and out of the hospital I started to make friends. Mary, Kara, and Heather were my main crew. We broke the rules by sharing phone numbers and we would get together on the weekends or after program was done. Even though I shouldn't have broken the rules, it helped me a lot. I needed a family and support so much at the time, and they became that for me. My family, people I learned to trust and respect. They knew my darkest secrets and didn't judge me. I wasn't a freak to them. All my friends that I knew prior to the incident had distanced themselves from me, which was very hard. But I was gaining something that I didn't realize at the time that I was gaining; hope. Hope where there was no hope before.

I also met a woman named Darlene during this time. At one point, Darlene had invited me to go to her house. We had been discussing the possibility of moving me into her house so that I could get out of the shelter and I went to her house to see if it would work for me.

While I was there I met her godson. Darlene had wanted to introduce me to him, because she said he was a lot of fun. When I met him, I asked him if we could go out.

"You want to go out tonight?" he asked me excitedly.

"Hell yeah!" I said. We all got ready and headed over to his place.

Darlene's godson was gay. I assumed that he lived with gay roommates, but one of those roommates was a female. We got to the house and everyone was drinking, so I had a glass myself. I also had a shot before they let me leave. I didn't drive because I was drinking, but I got into a car with people who were drinking without thinking twice about it. I didn't care I was drunk and was not thinking of the consequences. I sat on top of a girl's lap, not even thinking about where we were headed. I was with a bunch of gay men you would think I would have realized what kind of bar I was about to enter, but I was not prepared for it at all. I was totally blown away by what I saw that night. A bunch of skinny gay men holding shots in their underwear selling them. All I knew was I got a glass of something that was a pretty blue and I chugged it down. Then I had another, then I had some shots. I was toasted. By the end of the night I ended up throwing up all over the bathroom and driving home with a bunch of drunk people. It was a once in a lifetime experience. That was the only time in my life that I have gotten drunk like that or been to a party like that. And I didn't stop there.

I went back to the guy's house which was the girl's house well. She was gay as well. It was bed time and I followed her into her bedroom and had my first and only experience with a female. It was great. The next morning Darlene and I woke up, got dressed, and headed to program. I vomited again that morning before we got in the car. I'll never forget this experience. It was pretty interesting that day in group. Both Darlene and I were hung over and Mary and Heather knew it. That was one of the longest days of my life....but well worth every memory!!!

Mary was in her thirties, quite a bit older than me. At first I didn't like her but then she grew on me. I never told her that though. Mary was the first person in the program to give me her number. It was nice to have someone to talk to after program instead of going "home" and being totally isolated until the next day. I spent much of that time sleeping. Partially because there was nothing else to do, but also because the medication they had me on was very sedating. One day Mary surprised me by telling me that she had been praying for me. I didn't know Mary was saved, so it struck me as a little odd at first. I told her that I would pray for her as well.

Summer came around and families started to have barbeques. Mary invited me to a barbeque at her house to meet her family in Seekonk, which was about 30 minutes away. We went after program one day in June. Mary was very excited about introducing me to her sister Kathy. Kathy was a lot older than Mary, she was in her fifties. There were a lot of people at Kathy's house with a lot of different mental and physical health problems. It was a little overwhelming.

Kathy had custody of Mary's daughter Theresa who has depression and diabetes. She also had custody of one of her granddaughter's, Denise. Denise has cerebral palsy and was physically and mentally disabled. Zachary suffered from ADHD and Asperger's syndrome which is a form of autism. Kathy also lived with her husband Fletcher, her son Wally and Wally's girlfriend Tamara. Kathy also had a daughter Jenny who lived there with her three children, Zackary, Kadin, and Ceryn. Jenny has bipolar disorder and could not care for her Zackary so Kathy and Fletcher had legal custody of him. Mary lived there as well. Kathy described it as her dysfunctional functional family. During dinner, Kathy asked me a lot of questions about myself and my story. I remember Kathy saying to Mary "Boy I don't like many of your friends, but I really like her!!" That was nice to hear. Things progressed and my relationship with Mary begin to shift. Mary would often tell me that she was praying for me. I thought that was nice and told her the same. After all I was sure all of those people in the so called church I grew up in sure weren't so it felt good to know someone cared enough to pray.

One visit to Mary's lead into two, and then three. A few months later, I was a regular at Mary's house. I began to sleep over and Mary and I became best buds. Our friendship blossomed and we became inseparable. We went to church together, we ran errands together, and most important of all, we supported each other. It didn't matter what our mental illnesses were, we were a team, "Kaelee and Mary".

One of the reasons I began to spend more time at Mary's initially was because I decided that I had enough treatments from Pathways and decided that I was going back to school. I attended New England Institute of Technology in Warwick RI. I did very well at first. Then my grades became to slip and began to stay at Kathy's and Mary's even more.

Then Kathy began to get sick. At the time I was living with her more than at the shelter. I loved them as a family and they loved me. Kathy and I discussed the possibility of moving me in with her and the family in Seekonk Ma. It was about a half hour ride each way. When Fletcher, Kathy's husband, approached me about moving in, I knew everyone was on the same page, so I moved in and once again I had a new family. Mary and I made the trip several times back and forth from Fall River Ma, to Seekonk Ma. I moved in exactly December 24, 2008. Christmas Eve.

Christmas that year was magical. Kathy loved decorating for Christmas so the house was always beautiful. I woke up that Christmas to children who loved me, friends that supported me, and a God that had stayed faithful. Although I felt pain for not being able to celebrate with my foster family, I was happy because someone loved me regardless of my illness. Kathy and Fletcher loved me and Mary was one of my closest friends. I felt so grateful to be living with people who understood where I was in life and decided to give me a chance in spite of it.

I dropped out of school to help out with Kathy. My birth father was not happy because he gave me 1500 dollars towards school. I was disappointed that I let him down and couldn't get his money back. Things were a little tough for a while. He believed in me and gave me mercy, he gave me hope for a better relationship with him.

Only time would tell if Mary truly was my friend, sister, and supporter. Mary and her family became my family. It felt like God gave me back an identity. I belonged to a family again. Kathy and I became very close as well. She kept on telling me that I reminded her of their mother. We would sit around and drink coffee and talk and laugh for hours. Kathy's friends all took me in as another friend as well. It was nice. There was always someone stopping by for coffee, always someone to talk to.

Before I moved in, Kathy told me that I was not allowed to hurt myself in her house. Cutting was out the window as an option to deal with my issues if I was going to be under their roof. I agreed to this because I wanted to stay there so bad. I also had to pay rent, I wasn't going to be living with them for free. Moving out of the shelter was awesome. I was there for 21 months but now a new life lay before me.

Living with Mary and Kathy was a roller-coaster, there was so much going on at the house due to all the people who lived there and all of their different diagnoses. Dealing with so many different needs at once could get overwhelming and I would freak out and end up in the hospital. Basically whenever my stress got to a level that I could not tolerate it anymore, I would take a little vacation to the psych ward. I usually was in anywhere from two weeks to thirty days. I rarely got visitors which made me more depressed and suicidal than I was already. There were a few times that Mary came to visit, once with Heather. Those times were so nice, it helped a lot to have a friendly face in a place where there is little hope.

Once I was refueled I jumped back into the role I played. I was a caregiver to Denise and Mary. I helped take Kathy to chemo and other doctor's appointments. Her health started to really deteriorate. It scared me very much. I had extreme anxiety about losing her. I would yell out to God, "Oh no not again God, you just gave me a family! Please Lord don't take them away!!!!

A year after I moved in with Kathy and Mary, it was time to go to court to release the restraining order that my foster family had against me. The district attorney dropped the charges, however my parents said all the same boundaries still remained even though the restraining order had been lifted. They did not even hug me, they just spoke and then left. When I got in the car I broke down. I wailed and wailed. I was so confused. I did everything that was asked of me and beyond. I thought by doing treatment and taking medication that would show them how dedicated I was in my recovery. There was nothing. Kathy rubbed my back in the car and she calmed me down. We went for breakfast and drank coffee.

"It's okay Kaelee," she said as she leaned over her coffee. "It's not what you hoped for or expected, but you can't let it prevent you from moving on."

I looked at her, puffy-eyed and sniffly. My eyes felt like they were on fire and my nose was still a running, sloppy mess.

"You're not losing anything. If they can't forgive you, they're the ones who are losing, not you. If anything, you've gained family from this experience." She put her coffee down and reached for my hands. "Our family. It's time to move on, sweetie."

It was easier said than done, but she was right. I knew she was right, and I resolved to try.

It took a long time. There was always something coming up; anniversary days, birthdays, holidays. I would be so sad around those times that I often ended up requiring a hospitalization. I would send my foster parents cards with money for the boys. There never was a phone call, a card, or any acknowledgment that they even received them. However I would know they got the cards because the money was taken out of my account. They didn't want anything to do with me, but they sure helped themselves to the cash. I was so crushed. I had this amazing family and because of mental illness I couldn't be a part of it. How fair is that? I really struggled.

I was a bit promiscuous for a while. I would get into situations where I was sleeping with people because I thought that I would gain some kind of comfort, which I didn't. GOD seemed to always make his spirit known to me. I was so angry that I didn't make very wise decisions. I remember cursing at God because I was looking for love and was finding it in all the wrong places.

I wouldn't totally accept the love God had for me. Instead I stayed angry and numb and I slept with one of my co-workers more than once. Still I couldn't see what God had to offer me. I still attended church when it was convenient for my needs, but walking in sin and anger I couldn't see what God had to offer me. I stayed angry, but deep down inside I was so sad. Here I was a young woman longing for someone to hold me and tell me everything was going to be okay, yet I stood alone.

Whenever I felt like I couldn't live with the disease of mental illness I would find myself having a break down and going back to the hospital. It was comforting being with people who got it. It was where I found peace and where I found God. I always had my Bible with me. I would find myself falling in love with God all over again. But it ended there. I struggled to find the same time with God and peace with the Bible when I was not in a controlled environment.

Being a part of Pathways, and the experiences I had as a result of that gave me an identity. I had friends, people loved me, and I had a purpose. It didn't fix any of my real world problems, it just helped me cope with them better. Working through the painful memories of my past and learning how my behaviors not only affected me but the people around me helped some, but it wasn't enough. I had to accept that I was who I was and no matter how much medication I took, no matter how much I spoke with therapists, and no matter how hard things got I was not wanted by my minister parents. I had to accept my reality and move on. It was so painful but Mary, Kathy, and my many providers gave me the skills I needed to overcome and live in freedom from what was. It was never going to be the same as it was, but at least I knew I could make it.

Leaving Pathways meant I needed a new therapist. Pathways wanted me to have after care and they connected me with a woman named Donna Welles who was in Marshfield, Ma. I drove the hour ride from Seekonk, Ma to Marshfield, Ma. every week. I had some more DBT training with her for another year. I loved Donna. She had all white hair. She wore glasses. She listened.

Chapter 10

My Long Lost Love

I always had feelings for my first love…Jonathan. We grew up in church together from a very young age and we did all of the same things together. As we got older, we became junior members, and later on, senior members of our church. These roles came with big responsibilities. We began to teach Sunday School classes. I taught the third and fourth graders. He taught boys group. We sang in the worship team. We were at church together at least five days out of seven.

We started dating when I was fifteen and then again after we graduated. Jonathan and I were intimate with each other but we never went all the way, which is why I broke up with him. Mostly touching and groping and oral sex. Jonathan chose not to enter into that because of the respect he had for my foster dad. The relationship fizzled out and we lost touch.

Then when Facebook came around, I looked him up and gave him a call. It was like we never separated. I told Kathy about him and asked if he could come over. She said yes and it was on. After all those years, we were going to finally go all the way. He was so excited and so was I. We were adults now, and without my foster father in the picture we could do what we chose without fear. When he came to visit he came on his motorcycle. He stayed the night and left in the morning, after breakfast. We didn't have anywhere for him to sleep in the house so we slept in the trailer Kathy used for camping.

After that I felt like I was on top of the world. Here I was with this new family, and now I have the man in my life that I completely love. I didn't have to explain myself, because he was there during my childhood. Everything was all right in my life again.

Kathy and some of her friends told me that they didn't like him, but I couldn't see it. He was very cocky, and a know-it-all who didn't really know much of anything. I was complete in denial of him flirting with Kathy's niece Kayleigh when Jenny, Kathy's daughter tried to tell me about it. I thought that they were talking crap because they didn't like him. I kept it in the back of my mind, but couldn't see it as possible after all we had been through together.

About eight months later, the holidays came around. I stayed home in Seekonk with my family for Christmas morning. I then made my way to Jonathan's and we celebrated New Year's together.

That night, we were in his room lying on the bed when he got up and walked across the room. He picked up a small box from his desk.

"Do you want it?" he asked.

I started laughing. "Yes! Yes, of course I do!"

I was so excited. I was engaged! I could hardly sleep that night. When I awoke the next morning, one of the stones on my ring was missing. I should have realized it was a sign of what was to come, but we got it fixed and all was well again. I went back home and told Kathy and Mary and we celebrated my engagement.

We then discussed about moving in together and I said that was fine, but that we couldn't live in Lawrence because of all the bad memories. We agree and we found a place in Haverhill.

I gave my two weeks' notice at work, packed my things, and moved into a luxury apartment in Haverhill. The apartment had two bedrooms, two full bathrooms, a washer and dryer, a dish washer, a garbage disposal, a microwave, and a fridge. It was gorgeous. We signed a year lease and we made it through the first six months before we realized that we had bitten off more than we could chew. Part of the reason was due to the fact that, even though Jonathan was working full time, his income came whenever his boss felt like paying him. I was working but only part time, and it wasn't enough to cover the difference.

Once we realized that we were living outside of our means, we decided that we needed to break the lease. We started to lose everything after that, the furniture got repossessed, then the motor-cycle and truck. One mistake after another. We moved back into his room at his mom's house. It was on the third floor with no bathroom, we had to go to the first floor. It was not insulated either, it was just a bed in the room, a heater for the winter and a bunch of blankets. It was tough.

But I didn't let any of it bother me. I was so excited to be engaged and feel like I finally had a purpose again. There was one dark cloud on the horizon though, that bothered me even more than the material struggles we were going through. I couldn't help thinking about my foster dad. We had several conversations when I was living with them about my future wedding. We would joke around and dream. However my life and his promise had changed…

You Promised Me

We use to joke around about my special day
You said that you rather walk me down the aisle instead of marrying me
You would give me away
You were the first man in my life who never hurt me…
I miss your bear hugs, tickling of my knee
I even miss you horsing with me
You promised and now you choose not to be there.

And now I'm left with someone else.
A person I could never love as much as I love you!
You Promised...

My family from Seekonk was not all that thrilled. They supported me, but they kept telling me that I didn't have to marry him. They tried to be happy for me, but not one of them cared for him at all. They gave me a gift that they called a "husband thumper. It was a tire thumper, a bat basically, and they taped a sign on it as a joke. I laughed at the time, but kept it in the back of my mind as a bit of a warning.

After a few months of living at his mom's house, I started to become very angry over how our lives were turning out. Jonathan promised that he would renovate the third floor as a place to come home to relax, but he never even attempted it and I became to have doubts. He was co-dependent with his mother and totally content to be living at home with her.

His younger brother and girlfriend also lived there. We didn't all get along at first which caused even more tension in the house. It was not pleasant living there and I told him all the time that we needed to get out.

We were planning for the wedding, but there was no venue, no decorations, no invitations, nothing. But I was so in love with this "man" that I didn't care that we had nothing for a wedding. We were planning on having 100 guests and yet we had no minister lined up to marry us. I don't know what we were thinking.

Jonathan was not really concerned. I was working and saved five hundred dollars to buy a wedding gown. Jonathan's mother offered to pay for the food for the wedding. That was supposed be our wedding gift from her, which was a God send considering we were living on a limited budget. Then she found out that I bought a wedding dress and was so angry she said she wasn't going to cater the wedding. She felt that we had the money to cater the wedding if I had enough money to buy a wedding dress. I was totally beside myself. What made it worse was that Jonathan agreed with her, he took his mother side over his future bride. Jonathan and I had been through so much together. How could he turn on me like that? I didn't care what his mother thought. I was supposed to be his bride. He obviously felt like he needed to stick up for his mommy.

As he was yelling at me for buying a wedding dress I realized that he was not the man I needed him to be, never mind the man of God I wanted him to be. I should have known when he refused to go to church with me. He said that's not for him. He would come on occasion to make me happy but then went out the window as soon as mommy stepped in. That gave me all the ammunition I needed to break up with him and go back to Seekonk. I called home to Kathy and Fletcher and Fletcher came and got me in his truck.

You're Such a Liar

Since the day I left you I questioned myself for walking away from you
and yet in my heart I say I was wrong...
My heart aches for you

my tears roll down and you're not there
I miss the smell of your clothes
I miss the smile on your face
I miss how you held me so gently and comforted me in those hard times
I miss how we made love and the peace I felt with you
I dream of the make-up sex that was so touching
I miss cuddling with you on the couch
I miss arguing with you over the silly things in life
I miss picking up after you
I miss our days together
I miss cooking with you and learning new things
I'm hurting and yet I am so angry with you
You leave and have another girlfriends
You don't return my calls
You change your number and then lie about it
You ignore that I'm at your front door
you turn your back on me and walk away
I tell you I love you and I always will
then I go to pawn my ring after all is said and done
and yet I see what a fake a person you truly are
You gave me a fake ring!!
How dare call yourself a man
I hope the next girl is worth your while and maybe she'll mean more to you
Maybe she'll actually be special enough to receive a ring
a real one
You took advantage of my innocence and acted as if you truly loved me
You could have been a man about it and told me the truth
Instead I make myself look like an ass trying to benefit from it
I had to go on welfare just to make it by
You continue in life making money living at home with mama
No wonder why you will never amount to nothing in a relationship
You're a bastard and I am so done with the bull shit
go to hell for all I care…but always know that I love you

Chapter 11

The Destruction

I felt so stupid and embarrassed. I was very depressed and I ended up hurting myself when I got back home to Seekonk. I decided that I was going to take my life and I overdosed. I went to bed with Denise and I awoke the next morning. Again. No matter how hard I tried I just couldn't seem to kill myself. I told Kathy what I did and she brought me to the hospital. I felt like my whole my world was falling apart.

I was admitted to the hospital once again. When I called home to Kathy, she told me that I was not welcome back home. I understood why. It was very disrespectful to do what I did. What would have happened if Denise woke up and I was blue? That would have been so traumatic and she wouldn't have known what to do to save my life and she would have had trouble processing it. Luckily, I had recently reconnected with my Aunty Donna. I called her up and she offered me a place to stay. I really didn't want to move back home to the chaos, but I had no choice. It was either going back to where I came from, go live in a group home, or be homeless in a shelter.

After I was released from the hospital I took a cab back to Kathy's to pack my stuff. Before I left I had spoken to my aunt about my mom.

"I told your mom that you're coming to live with me Kaelee, I hope you don't mind. I told her I don't want any shit over it."

"Okay." I knew she would find out anyway, but I wasn't sure how I felt about it yet.

"She says good. She prefers for you to be with me, thinks it's better anyway. She is coming to pick you up at Kathy's house with your sister. I just thought I should prepare you for it."

"Thanks Aunty."

My sister and mother came in a big SUV to pick me and my belongings up. I moved home to Aunty Donna in January of 2011. I was really messed up and she was so supportive.

When I moved in with my aunt, her husband wasn't there. I barely knew him, I had met him briefly at my sister's twin's funeral. She told me Uncle Paul was in treatment in Bridgewater,

Massachusetts. I asked her why and she told me that he got caught up with an undercover officer with drugs.

The bid he was doing for the drug charge was five years. I never thought in a million years that I would visit another man in a jail. Well, all that went out the window when I moved in with Aunty Donna. I went to her and told her I wanted to meet him. Before we went to visit him, Aunty Donna had told him all about me, so it wasn't as awkward as expected it to be. Uncle Paul gave me a hug, and we sat down and got some goodies out of the vending machine. We sat for five hours just talking. We left and I told aunty on the drive home that I liked him and he made me feel comfortable. We tried to visit once a week for two years after that, although sometimes it was less in the winter. I became close to my Uncle Paul during this time.

Chapter 12

Rebuilding

When I moved into my Aunty Donna's house, we sat down and discussed how much my rent would be. She said she would charge me $400 a month with everything included. At the time my Uncle Moses lived with her, and one of her friend's sons lived there too. One big happy family we were not. Things in the house were tense. My uncle Moe lived on the couch and he had all kinds of medical issues. He had bad legs, so he used a urinal to pee in at night time. The boy living upstairs across from me smoked a lot of weed and he was dirty. My aunt smoked too. In my mind all I could think was, great, here we go again. My friend Kathy from Seekonk encouraged my aunt to get me on Social Security and I started the process in late January of 2011. I ended up back in the hospital around March of that year.

The team that was working with me noticed that I was not progressing with regular treatment. After much discussion and assurance by the medical team that it was a good decision for me, I agreed to go in for shock therapy. I was taken to a different hospital for the treatment and I would lay down on a stretcher. The nurse would put little electrodes all over my head and they would put me to sleep. They placed a guard of some sort in my mouth. I'm not sure how long I was under but when I regained consciousness, it felt like I got run over by a truck. Now on top my range of psych meds I was also taking anti-nausea pills to prevent getting sick, Tylenol for body aches and fever. The purpose of ECT was to erase the negative images of my past and put them back in my subconscious, so that my Post Traumatic Disorder (PTSD) would be less intrusive. That would help me to control my emotions and how I reacted to the world around me.

I had six rounds of therapy before I was released. I was completely different when it was over, but not in a good way. The treatments made me feel like a zombie. I could not put sentences together and I was talking incoherently. I couldn't remember my therapist. It was stressful going to therapy and not remembering who she was and the things we were working on. I knew who the people around me were, but I couldn't have extensive conversations with them. My poor aunt took me to go see my uncle and I told him that he had a big nose. I don't remember it, but they told me about it after. My uncle laughed at me and then yelled at aunty for allowing me to go through with it. After therapy was over, I went back to my day to day activities and after a while I began to be myself once again. It was really weird when I got out of the hospital because I couldn't put my thoughts together in order to respond to the things around me. Everything was really slow and it took me a while to recover. Shock therapy did nothing to help me with forgetting or suppressing my memory. If anything, it made it worse in some aspects. For instance, when I would have a flash black, instead of it going through my body and ending quickly, everything was in slow motion. This caused me great distress and I would cut to cope. Hearing voices increased my symptoms and I was hearing them more than ever.

After being discharged from the hospital where I was getting the ECT, they set me up with a partial hospitalization program at Aubore counseling in Haverhill, Ma. The program would last one week to three weeks at the most. I didn't have a car because I totaled it on the highway one day while I was on my way to see my counselor in Marshfield, Ma. The director of the program at Aubore called me and set up a ride for me with a woman named Bev to pick me up and drop me off after program. I became very close with her and I was glad to make another friend.

One of the things that the program offered was an initial sit down with a clinician for 45 minutes to evaluate you, figure out why you were there and what symptoms you were having. This were I met Jean Smith. She was an older woman and one of the therapists at the center. I remember talking with her and asking her if she was taking new clients. She was. I was so relieved because I liked Jean right from the start and it meant I didn't have to go hunting for a therapist.

One thing that was very unique about Jean was that she is legally blind. This was a problem for me. It actually helped me to realize that there nothing in this world that I cannot do. Jean has proven over and over again that anything is possible. She has visited Cape Cod to visit with her daughter and family. She has two grandsons. She uses public transportation by herself. She has no problem asking for assistance when she is out and about when she needs it. Since I been working with Jean she has been to Russia, Italy, Europe, and Africa. She goes anywhere and does anything her heart desires. There are no limits for her. She encourages me to never give up my dream of becoming a registered nurse. Her mother was registered nurse who never allowed Jean to be less than anyone else. She always made a way. Jean portrays a positive attitude and offers a different alternative to any situation that I might have in front of me. She has helped me with some really tough situations and made a big difference in my life.

We had been working together for a couple of months before I had ECT shock therapy, but I had forgotten about it since the ECT messed up my short term memory. Jean would help me get through the emotions and helped me process the emotions and behaviors that followed. Although she couldn't see me she had this way of connecting to the little girl inside who was still hurting. Jean would lean forward in her chair and grab my hand to console me. I was totally surprised the first time it happened, and it was when I realized that God's promise to keep me close to his heart was true. In that moment it felt like the Lord reached down from heaven and touched me. I was so overwhelmed by it. God had to send me someone who couldn't see to show me that hope is real and it was not just for certain people. His grace is enough for everyone. His grace is enough for me.

In July of 2011 I received my first disability check. I paid my debts and went shopping for some things that I needed. I bought a computer, clothes, and shoes. Since I couldn't find work right away, I stayed on disability while I got treatment for my illness. I continued to work with my counselor Jean and my psychiatrist Rachel. They continued with my care, and they both agreed and concluded that I suffer from Post-traumatic stress disorder and bipolar disorder. After all those years of treatment and continued support, it was official. I finally had an answer as to what I have been dealing with all these years. Now, I have learn how to live with it.

Later on that year, I was having a mood swing; a severe low and I was suicidal. I went to Jean's office and I was a wreck.

"Kaelee, I think we need to get you some help."

"I don't want help. I don't need help. I'm done getting help." I responded.

"Why did you come here to see me then, if you don't want help?"

This sent me into a rage.

"Fuck off! You don't know me! You don't know what's going on! If I say I don't want help, it means I don't want help!" I stormed out of her office and went to the grocery store and bought a drink. I had a bottle of anxiety medication, Vistril, in my purse. I left the store and downed 25 capsules of my medication and angrily started to walk back toward Methuen.

My Aunt Donna caught up with me in a McDonald's parking lot. I got in the car and told her what I did. She immediately brought me to the emergency room. She walked me in and told the receptionist what I did. They brought me to a room right away to check me over. I was put on cardiac monitors while they took some blood and urine tests. At this point I knew the whole protocol. What I didn't know was that Vistril similarly to Benadryl. It puts you to sleep. I fell asleep and the staff allowed me to sleep throughout the night. In the morning they brought me to an adult psychiatric floor. Here we go again, by now I was so used to it that it had become my normal. They straightened out my meds and I went home about two weeks later.

When I was released from the hospital, I had a new referral. I was contacted by a woman named Ann Byron from an agency called Vinfen. It is a facility that cares for people who have a psychiatric issues. They are there to create goals for you and to help you meet those goals. They are a good sounding board for me, and I see clinicians regularly throughout the month. There are three that I work closely with. Ann Byron, Jennifer Roberts and Christine Kelly. I have worked with other providers but they come and go. They have helped me through some tough times, but there also are there when I'm well. They had nominated me for a special reward, Achievement of Recovery. It means that I have come to meet my goals and continue to do so. These women have been my angels. I am very grateful for this service.

Things at Aunty Donna's were rough. She was very up my butt all the time. She had a lot of good reasons. The voices in my head were demanding and at times really overbearing at that time. She had to start giving me my medication because they kept on telling me not to take them, or take them all. Aunty got to know me like a hawk. She knew just by how I said good morning what my day was going to be like. I would get so annoyed because she knew me better than I knew myself. That was very intimidating.

She would tell me you have that "don't give a shit" attitude. We would fight.

At one point, we were driving in North Andover, Ma. We were arguing about the same stuff as usual when Aunty turned to me.

"If you don't like what I have to say then get out of my car!" We were stopped at a stoplight and she pointed outside as she said this.

"I will!" I shouted back and I opened the door just as the light turned green and got out. I started walking down the sidewalk in the opposite direction as I heard Aunty slam the car door behind me. She turned around and pulled up beside me.

"Kaelee, get back in the car." I kept walking. "Where are you going to go Kaelee? Come on, just get back in the car. This is ridiculous."

I turned around and crossed the street. Aunty had to turn the car around again, she wasn't just going to let me go even though I wanted her to. I got mad and started to run. Aunty pulled the car ahead of me and drove it up the curb into some lady's front yard. She was grabbing her chest and breathing hard. I walked up to the window.

"Stop being dramatic Aunty, you're fine."

"No, I'm not," she half gasped. "You're giving me an anxiety attack!"

I watched her for a minute and then realized she was telling the truth. She started to get it under control and I was overcome with regret.

"I'm so sorry Aunty," I half mumbled. "I love you Aunty, I really don't know what I would do without you."

"I love you too Kaelee, that's why I'm so hard on you," she gasped, still getting over her anxiety attack a little. "Now get in the damn car, will you?"

I walked around and climbed in and we drove off again. Aunty was right. I was out of control. This time, instead of going in-patient all over again, I went back to the partial hospitalization at Arbor in Haverhill where Jean and Rachel worked because that had worked well for me. Going through the program again, and working with people I trusted, was like a reset for me. After that I was ok, back on my medication and not playing doctor anymore.

2011 went by fast. After that episode my first holiday season home in eleven years began. It was really overwhelming. I liked seeing my niece and nephews open their presents, and I survived the rest. I hate the holidays because they were so painful growing up but also as an adult. However this Christmas was good. It was the first time home with birth family and this Christmas Aunty Donna, myself, Myrakel, and my sister Jessica. And for the next three that's what we did. For the most part Myrakel basically lived with aunty and I. Jessica came and went as she pleased. Aunty and I were fine with that.

Myrakel is very special to me. Jessica has three sons, one single and the twins, but they all died in utero. Myrakel's birth was very difficult, however after a lot of heart ache, she came on January 10, 2009. My sister had to get a C-section and I was the one to go in the operating room with her because my mother was too large to fit in the scrubs. I was the first one to touch her, pray over her, bless her, and carry her. It was an amazing experience. I tell Myrakel all the time that we are close because she is just like me, and it's the truth. She reminds me of myself all the time. She laughs and calls me crazy aunty.

That Christmas, with the help of Aunty Donna she bought me a shirt that stated "beware of my crazy aunty". It was so funny. She had given me hints for weeks as to what it was. I knew that it was a shirt and the color.

"See aunty, you *are* crazy," she got out just before she started to laugh hysterically. I love being an aunt to both Myrakel and my brother's son, Jeffery. I'm not as close to my other nephew. I remember his birthday and Christmas, but that's pretty much all.

After the holidays of 2011, I stopped surviving. When I went to go see Jean she would push me to work through my issues, when I didn't really want to. I was cutting and there was no one stopping me. Part of me wanted them to stop me, but I couldn't stop myself and there was nothing they could do. I would cut in the shower, patch it all up, and then text Jean and aunty and tell them that I hurt myself. I was out of control; a bomb ready to explode.

Chapter 13

What Was I Thinking?

I got through the first part of 2012 without being hospitalized, but that didn't mean I was doing well. I wasn't through the darkness yet. I got overwhelmed again and I stopped taking my medication. I was in a manic episode but I was suicidal again also. I remember I had Myrakel in my room one day. We were doing what she loves to do most, painting our nails. She panted mine, it was adorable. I took pictures of her painting because it was a good memory, and I wanted to save it. In my mind I was saying good bye to her and thinking that at least her last memory of me would be doing her favorite thing with aunty.

I thought about my family down in Seekonk and I made a trip down. This was in October of 2012. I was so out of control that I got into a fight with Kathy and the others that were in the house. After the fight, we went out for karaoke and I sang a couple of songs. I went to the bathroom and cut myself to get through the night, and kept it hidden. One of Kathy's friends does tattoos, and I ironically had a bible verse tattooed onto my right leg. I was acting impulsively, I was so angry and out of sorts. Aunty Donna and I got into a huge fight before I went to Seekonk that night. She was begging me to stay home because Uncle Paul was really sick and he was in the hospital. The jail could not tell her where he was for security reasons and she wanted me there. He ended up getting four pints of blood. He was severely sick, but I was too selfish and self-absorbed to care. I figured there was nothing I could do to change it and couldn't see why it was so bad to go to Seekonk. I know now how selfish I was by going, but I also know how desperate I felt as well. I came home at the end of the weekend and went back into the hospital.

I walked the halls with my head down, struggling with my voices. The staff was trying to stabilize me to get me out of there so I could recuperate with my regular providers.

"Hello, how are you?" I heard a man speak to me as I walked past. I looked up and there he was. Jacob. Jacob was a bigger man with the face of a cutie pie. I was beside myself, instantly attracted. Jacob and I began to talk about our lives and the different experiences that we had gone through in the past. It was heart breaking to hear some of what he had gone through, my heart went out to him. I wanted to make it all better, to heal this man. Never mind the fact that I still had so much healing to do myself.

"Look, I have something to say to you. I want to be honest and upfront now, while we are getting to know each other."

"Okay," I replied, not sure what to expect.

"I'm a level two sex offender. With everything you've already been through, it's something you should know."

I took a deep breath. Of course. Here I was, talking to a man who had done the one thing that offended me the most, the type of man my mother would have dated and introduced me to, the type of man I swore I would never be attracted to.

"I was eighteen, and she was fifteen. She told me she was older and I stupidly believed her. Her sister found out and told their mother and she took me to court. I went to jail for it, and it's on my record forever."

My mind was going a million miles an hour. I should have turned around and run as fast as I could in the other direction. But for some reason I didn't. I called my aunt and told her all about him.

"Aunty, you always tell me to give things a chance. Do you think we can give him a space to stay until he gets back on his feet? He's been through so much."

"If you feel like it is the right thing to do, Kaelee, I would need to talk to your Uncle Paul about it first, but we can probably figure something out." I mouthed to Jacob, "She said yes!"

As I hung up the phone, there was patient who was suffering from alcohol tremors who fell head first on to the concrete floor. I immediately jumped into nursing mode and got him on his back and supported his head. I yelled to Jacob to push the emergency button. The staff came right in. It was such a rush and the staff was amazed at how I handled the situation. This really helped me to realize that I need to be in nursing because I have skills and abilities that not everyone has.

I was released that Friday and Jacob came home the following Monday. Once he came into the house I noticed that he only had a back pack on.

"Do you have enough clothes in there?" I asked him. "It looks pretty small."

He shrugged. "Not really. I basically only have the clothes I'm wearing right now."

I knew he needed more than that, so I went to aunty and she gave him some of her old sweatpants, shirts, and sweatshirts. He told me that he felt more loved than he had in a long time. That night we had sex. It was only ok, but that didn't stop me from allowing things to continue.

Uncle Paul would call from jail and he would ask if Jacob was there. Aunty told him that he took the bus home at first, but Uncle Paul was no dummy and he knew better. She then told him that Jacob was staying there, but told Uncle Paul he was contributing. Aunty told him that he would have to pay her $400 a month to stay. Jacob only had welfare and food stamps, so Aunty Donna would take half his check from welfare and all of his food stamps to cover his rent.

Then we decided to help get him onto Social Security. He eventually did and he used his first check to pay Aunty Donna what he owed her and then he bought himself a $600 game system with the rest. I was pretty pissed off about that, because I had been covering him for his essentials and clothes while also trying to take care of myself. I thought he should buy his own stuff with the money instead of leaving it to me. I told him but he didn't care.

A few months after Jacob moved in with us I found out he had not been entirely truthful with me. We were out and we ran into an old friend of his who went to beauty school with my sister. A week later, she told my sister that when he was eleven years old he was caught raping his little sister. . I confronted him on it, and told him if he told me the truth then I would not get mad at him, and he told me.

"Oh my God," I thought. "What am I doing?" I didn't think it would be true, I didn't want to believe it was true until he told me. I had promised to not get mad. Here I was, repeating my mother's mistake. I was determined to fix it though. I took him to church with me. He became a Christian and got baptized.

I thought it was over at that point, however Jacob had another secret. He loved to smoke pot and drink alcohol. At the time, my aunt was a smoker as well and he would buy it off her. I would go to bed around nine, and he would tuck me in and go to the next door neighbor's house and party with them all night. I didn't mind that so much, they were all grown men and had the right to make those choices for themselves. What bothered me was the financial side. Now that he had a little money, he would spend it all on weed. This is what really pissed me off. Whenever we went out I had to pay, which usually meant I had to borrow money from my aunt and pay her back later. It was a nasty vicious cycle that continued for months.

Then we found out that Jacob had been going through my aunt's room and stealing pot as well. She would move it, but he was going through all the things in her room until he found it. She brought it to my attention one day and I confronted him on it. He denied it at first, but eventually told me the truth. So Jacob was a thief, a liar, a pot head, a drinker, and a bum. He would stay home all day and all night and play video games on his PlayStation. When he wasn't smoking pot and drinking at the neighbor's house that is. It was brutal. I was working to bring some money home and trying to make my life better while I had this grown man at home doing absolutely nothing with his life and letting me take care of him.

In the meantime my uncle Paul came home from prison, which was awesome. We had been waiting for him to come so long and we were all excited to have him home again.

I started to realize that Jacob was not even close to what I wanted out of life, and he certainly wasn't the type of man I had hoped for. I started to think about breaking up with him. I confided in my aunt first.

"Aunty, I don't think Jacob is the right man for me. I think maybe I have made a mistake."

"Kaelee, if that's how you feel. Maybe you should try giving him another chance though. He still could change."

"He's not going to change. But I don't know how to do it. How do we get him out of here? He has no place to go."

"Give him a chance Kaelee, you never know what's going to happen."

Then the problem resolved itself. In January of 2014 Jacob decided to take my aunt's car, the only car we had for all of us at the time. He got into a severe accident and hit four cars. He called me.

"Kaelee, I'm all fucked up."

"What do you mean? I thought you were at the neighbor's house."

"I took the car, and I got into a car accident."

"Stop lying. You're next door."

No, seriously."

"Where are you?"

"I'm in Haverhill, I got into an accident with the car."

"You did what?"

"No, Kaelee, I'm for real. Listen." He turned the ignition on and I could hear the engine pinging. "The police and ambulance are coming. I'm hurt. Tell Aunty Donna and Uncle Paul."

I hung up and I ran down stairs to tell my aunt and uncle. Aunty got on the phone and called the police and reported it stolen. Jacob and I lasted 18 months of moment by moment anxiety, what I thought was the rest of my life. That night we were over though, and I was glad to be done with him. He never was arrested but had to go to court for what he did. We said that we didn't want him to go to jail, but we wanted him to be punished. The court gave him fines and probation.

That chapter of my life was over and I never felt so relieved in all of my life. There was a purpose, God and my aunt have showed me that love has no boundaries as long you try it first. I don't recommend to go out and find a sex offender to live with, I've heard many stories that my uncle has told me about the kind of men he lived with in jail. Pretty scary. But I learned from it. I vowed I would never be with a sex offender after what my mother put me through, but I did. This doesn't make me like her. My mother went out with known child predators and let them live with us when we were young children. Everyone knew but couldn't do anything about it. They would ask me about it, but I never told them because fear is so paralyzing. My mother has said she liked it because of all the stuff she got out of it. She called me a liar for years when I told her and others what was going on. She said I was jealous of the younger girls who Manny was paying more attention to because I was getting too big for him. I am not and never will be like her.

My aunt and uncle got a new car. I had to go to my father and ask him to buy me a car, and help me insure and register it. The car he ended up buying was a piece of crap that barely got around, but I got lucky. I was hit by another car on an on ramp to the highway and I got more money back than what I bought the car for. My uncle and aunt took me to buy a new one with the money I got back from the insurance. I had some money left over to put a payment on the money I owed my father for the original car. I was so happy, I had a better car and less debt. I finally had some independence. I can now get into my car and go where ever I want to. I can pay my own gas and not have to worry about being home in time for my aunt and uncle to use the car.

Chapter 14

New Beginning

I changed the color of my room from yellow to purple, Uncle Paul painted it for me. My friend Polly gave me a lot of ideas for what to do with my furniture to make what I had different. She was a very strong person for me. I met her in church and she was determined that my relationship with Jacob would not turn out like her relationship with her ex-boyfriend, who still lives with her. She felt like helping me move on would keep him, or someone worse, from coming back. Polly has become one of my closest friends.

I also have great support from a group of women who stand my side. They are helping me to heal and become the woman I want to be. Other than Polly, there is Kristen, Christen, Laureen, and Sally. These women are Bible based God fearing women and I love each and every single one of them. I see them all weekly. It's a sisterhood that I have fallen into and love. The greatest thing about my girlfriends is sharing the joy of the Lord in our hearts. Even though I named these five women specifically, there are many more relationships that I have developed with people that are helping me to heal. They share the same goals and values as I do and it is really great having them in my life.

I wanted to volunteer for hospice so I went through a course and I now volunteer at the Hospice House. This led me to a per diem job as a certified nursing assistant. I loved this job and I got really close to one patient in particular. I would come in early just to squeeze some extra time with her. Unfortunately, her mother didn't have that warm spirit towards me and claimed that I was being rough with her daughter. I wasn't, and I tried to defend myself, but I was told I couldn't work with her any longer. I was heartbroken. Unfortunately another patient there complained when I was in taking care of him and his cell phone dropped on the floor when I moved the table. He complained that I was too loud and I felt like it was time to move on.

I applied to work in a nursing home after leaving the hospice and I was hired on the spot. That was July 2014. I worked and I earned every penny. It wasn't easy work. I started to really think about what I wanted to do with my future and I looked into becoming a medical assistant. I needed to go to school and ended up choosing for The Salter School in Tewksbury, Ma. My begin date was September 08, 2014. I quit my job since I had my social security to pay my bills and I had a stable home life with my aunt and uncle. I could focus entirely on school with no distractions.

There were five modules that you had to complete in six week segments. I started in September, but then had to take six weeks off in order to help my aunt when she had her right knee replaced. When I went back to school I was in a new class, which was a relief because the class that I was originally with was very loud and there was a lot of tension. The staff had a hard time with them and it was very hard for me too. My new class was awesome, very friendly and helpful. I was hospitalized again at the end of May due to voices and mania, but I jumped through hoops and got back to school within a week. It did not affect my performance at school. Many of my class-mates were concerned and hit me up on the computer. It was nice to feel cared about by them and helped me to complete school successfully.

I finished all my classes got an externship at an OBGYN office, in Wilmington, Massachusetts. Debbie the office manager showed me how to set up the room and clean it between patients and I learned how to assist the doctor in handling the instruments. It was amazing to hear the heart-beat of a baby in the womb for the first time and I will never forget it. I can't wait until the day I can hear my own baby's heartbeat. I learned a lot there and I am forever grateful. I didn't think I would like working for an OBGYN, but I ended up loving it. It taught me the importance of trying something out first because you might end up liking it. Unfortunately the practice was not hiring, and I had to leave when my externship was over.

A week before my sister□s fiancé got out of jail he became religious and it hurts me very deeply to watch my niece get brain washed by his ideas. It's not the religion that is the problem as much as it is the new rules that started when he came home. Myrakel is no longer allowed over to Aunty Donna and Uncle Paul's house where I live, and I now have to make an appointment to see her because of problems her husband had with Uncle Paul. The holidays are so painful now because we aren't celebrating together, and having Myrakel there is what made the holidays enjoyable for me.

There are other problems that have come up now that they have converted. My sister, her friends, and I went to the bridal shop in order to get fitted and to place a down payment on our gowns. I didn't have the money and my sister took care of me for that moment. She then gave a little speech about how thankful she was for me, and she added at the end that all her brides-maids will be wearing a hijab. I thought about it on the way home and realized I was not com-fortable with it.

I called her when I got home.

"Jessica, I would love to be in the wedding, but I am not comfortable wearing a hijab. I'm sorry, but I've thought it over and I can't do it."

"Seriously Kaelee? It's not even that big of a deal and it's important to me. Do you even care about that? It's always all about you! This is my wedding and no one else has a problem with it. What am I going to do, make everyone else wear one, and not you? Is that fair?"

I didn't say anything, just let her rant for a few minutes. But then she said something I never expected to hear.

"You know what, if that's how you feel, fine. You aren't part of my wedding anymore." She hung up.

I was hurt by her decision, but I knew she only asked me because I☐m her only sister and she wanted some family support other than our mother. She tried to say that was because of her fiancé and yes it was, but not for the reason she said. The truth is, he doesn't like me any more than I like him.

I had Myrakel and Jeffrey on different occasions throughout that summer, but my sister did not talk to me for months. I had and still have to get Myrakel from my mother if I want to see her. It gets complicated. Jessica drops Myrakel at my mother's house, I pick her up, and then drop her off at my mother's house when I'm done. My sister picks her up from there and brings her home. It's a pretty sucky set up but it works.

My sister was married on September 6 of 2015. That day came and went for me uneventfully as I still wasn't invited. When she put pictures of the wedding up on Facebook, I was in total disbelief. Not one of her bridesmaids was wearing a hijab. I was so hurt. She didn't really want me there, it was all a ploy to get me out. That was the second time that summer that my whole entire birth family was together and not one of them reached out to me, the first being Jeffrey's birthday.

The pain of it all really hurts. I cry in my car as it is the only place where I can be alone and really get it all out. I realized recently for the first time that all of the relationships I have had over my life have led to deep sadness. I was the attractive little girl that all my mother's boyfriends had fun with. There was Manny, whose abuse caused me lifelong trauma. The Smiths, who promised to love me no matter what, but could not stick in there for the long haul. Kathy, who did all she could do to help me, but she too had to let me go. Kathy died November 25, 2015 of pancreatic cancer.

All of my friends that I knew growing up in the Salvation Army all left as soon as my parents left. I was left to be alone. When I was alone, Jesus came into my heart and cleansed me. He promised me in his word that he would never leave me nor forsake me. He has helped me hold on and move forward.

I am 29 years old and I have been hospitalized 29 times for psychiatric issues. I have had the privilege to gain coping skills that I was not given as a child through my many experiences. I could have and arguably should have been in the streets doing drugs and possibly prostituting because of the environment I was raised in. But God reached his arms down and put certain people my path in order for me to rise up and be called his child.

I was locked in fear for many years. Being a child locked in fear silences that little voice inside you. My mother would make us lie to Aunty Donna for whatever reason. I learned that to shut my mother up, you would do anything to not get into trouble or even a beating, so I lived a life of lies, a life of prostituting, molestation, neglect and abuse. I learned to stay silent. ....

With God reaching down and scooping me into his presence on so many occasions and protecting me against myself, I am no longer a slave to fear for I am a child of God. I no longer stay silent. Peace has surround me with his love. I am redeemed, I am a princess, I am a believer, I am raised up. God has truly restored my soul. I go to church weekly and I live my life away from fear. To all my abusers out there who thought that I would stay where I came from, I have risen from the demons of my past. I am risen up.

There is still hope out there. Don't be silenced. I lived in hell my first thirteen years of my life, then through severe disappointment of losing everything and everyone I used to know in my twenties. Now I will be turning 30 years old and I have dreams and goals. I am focused. I have a host of angels that are my friends and my aunt and uncle that have supported me. God has restored me. I will not be silenced again. God has given us all choices and you have the choice to be locked away in silence or come out and be bold and stop the cycle of abuse. There are so many agencies, hospitals, support groups, therapists. With God all things are possible, don't be silenced.

Silence is the devil's avenue to use voices, hallucination, self-doubt, anger, pain, and suicide to control your life. I have attempted to overdose three times. I look back and it all makes sense, since I walked in silence for 21 years. Yes I spoke of the sexual abuse, I tried to yell for help during my teen years with cutting. But no one really knew the horror I felt inside my body and the devil got ahold of me and took over my life for many years. With these experiences I have learned to have a voice. It's scary to come out and tell people what is really going on in your head, but the moment you do is the moment that you choose to break the cycle of abuse and give insight to your mental illness. That's when you find freedom.

Coming out gave me the power to live. I passed my test for registered medical assistant. I am writing this book and getting it published. I am fulfilling my goals and dreams. I have more to come and I'm finally on the right path to completing them. One of my biggest dreams is to meet Mr. Right, get married and have children. I'm working towards my childhood dream of becoming a registered nurse. I'm looking forward to going sky diving someday and traveling to different countries. I want to travel to Africa as a missions nurse to work with children dying from AIDS. I want to live for God and do whatever he wants me to serve his needs here on Earth.

Live your dreams and never look back unless you need to in order to find strength to move forward. Silence does not have to be your only option. Scream at the top of your lungs, run as fast as you can, cry as loud and hard as your body allows; but don't ever live in silence. For me God is my strength and my guide. I hope this book encourages you to never stay silent.

CPSIA information can be obtained at www.ICGtesting.com
Printed in the USA
BVOW04s0740260416

445579BV00002B/2/P